LEGITIMATE

Faith

LEGITIMATE

Faith

...producing Authentic Hope!

∾

JOE SCHOFIELD

Printed in the United States of America

ISBN 978-1-958434-74-1 (paperback)
ISBN 978-1-958434-76-5 (hardback)
ISBN 978-1-958434-75-8 (ebook)

LCCN: 2022923735

Self-Help; Religion; Autobiography

MainSpring Books
5901 W. Century Blvd
Suite 750
Los Angeles, CA, US, 90045
www.mainspringbooks.com

DEDICATIONS

To the most wonderful parents a man
could ever be blessed with . . .

Jean and Don Schofield

I Love You

* * * * *

CONTENTS

MY WONDERFUL CHILDREN

I am especially thankful and grateful for my children. God blessed me with each of you, taught me through each of you, and forever shows His love for me in my relationship with you! There is no prouder father in the entire world than I am.

Amy Jo-God bless you as you sing and write for Him. You are such a godly woman and countless people are growing close to the Savior through your music and leadership ministry. Squeeze hunter; Carter and Taylor for Pa Pa Joe!

Courtney-you are a special woman of God and I will always remember the times we shared watching God work in your life. Keep singing for Him and touching the lives around you with His love . . . and hug precious little Ruby for Pa Pa Joe!

John Roger-You've got the music in you, Son, and a heart that feels for everyone. You write, hear and help all who know you! Thank you for being my wonderful son and for the precious bond we have and will ever share . . . Daddy/Dude days forever!

* * * * *

ENDORSEMENTS

In the years Joe Schofield had served as our Minister to Senior Adults at Prestonwood Baptist Church, he has endeared himself to those of us who sit under his teaching, and also to others among the congregation having had the opportunity to come to know him.

With his kind spirit and effective teaching skills, Joe brings the Scriptures to life each week in the Encouragers class. We look forward to every lesson, knowing that we will receive God's Word in a way that will encourage us to apply the Scriptures to how we live our lives every day, whether in the church, in the community, or in the home.

We are privileged to see Joe Schofield make the application of Biblical principles to his own life. Joe equips his Bible students with the tools necessary to live victorious Christian lives and models the application of God's Word before us.

Thank you, Joe, for allowing the Lord to work in and through you. We appreciate you!

Zig Ziglar
Author and Motivational Teacher

* * * * *

* * * * *

Joe Schofield's *Legitimate Faith* is a message lived out on the anvil of his life. I have known Joe for over 35 years as a man of joyous faith and confident hope. If you want your faith to be real and relevant, read this book.

Jack Graham
Pastor, Prestonwood Baptist Church
Plano, Texas

* * * * *

In your spiritual journey, you meet a few rare individuals who really stand out and shine the love of Jesus onto everyone around them Joe Schofield is one of those marvelous "lights" for the Kingdom of Christ! His book, *Legitimate Faith* is filled with the life experiences of a man who has traveled the Christian road of life and survived many bumpy roads because of his enduring faith. You will laugh at the scores of hilarious stories and illustrations and most of all learn how a legitimate and genuine faith is lived using God's Word as a guide through the dark valleys that we often travel in this sinful world. Joe and I have a lot of common experiences in the ministry and I can honestly tell you that Legitimate Faith will be a great source of inspirations and strength to all Christians who are seeking to walk closer with our Lord and Savior Jesus Christ! This book is a "must have" for every Christian's library!

Rix W. Tillman, D. Min
Past President of the Southern Baptists of Texas Convention
and author of "Pastor Survival" and "Time Sequence Bible"

* * * * *

Joe Schofield is a living example of authentic Christian leadership! During his tenure at Grapevine Faith, students, parents, and staff were enriched as he poured daily words of affirmation into each person through real-life stories. Joe's passion for people becomes evident to the reader as his life stories communicate both God's Amazing Grace and our Blessed Assurance in *Legitimate Faith*.

Ed C. Smith, Ed. D.
President, Grapevine Faith Christian School
Grapevine, Texas

INTRODUCTION

I wrote a song once that had a particular line that has stuck in my mind! It sad, *"Lookin' back through that tunnel of time, I've come to find that I'm not missin' you."*

I have written this book which is a story of my life with the realization that legitimate faith comes from life when we are willing to learn from God each day . . . and discover later that the person He is molding us to be, will never *"miss"* the one that is left behind. You see, *"Legitimate Faith"* always produces a living *"Authentic Hope."* Through the difficult years of my life I have come to a deeper understanding of that "Hope" In Christ Jesus!

Pascal said, *"All the good maxims have been written. It only remains to put them into practice."* This book is my personal witness to the power of faith and hope in Christ through disobedience, pain, frustrations, unexpected adversity and human weakness. God's faithfulness was unbelievable proof of the old song, "Through It All."

"Lookin' back through that tunnel of time," has shown me the living faith that God has molded in my heart. No longer do I as a young Christian believe black ink on white paper in my Bible, which seemed like theory, but I believed by young faith. Those words have jumped off the page and have become reality, instilling themselves in my very being. "Only God" is now an axiom of experience and belief, rather than a quote to remember!

I thank Him for those precious people in my life, family and friends in ministry, that have communicated that "legitimate faith and authentic hope" to me . . . making it possible for God to grip, mold and at times nearly suffocate me through my mistakes to become locked into His call daily!

My prayer is that you will be able to see **His faithfulness** and **authentic hope** through my frailties and failures, and in doing so, allow Him to enlighten, redirect and empower your life even today! As Pascal said, "Put them into practice!"

Joe Schofield

Chapter One

Do I Understand What Faith Is?

I remember as a nine year-old boy repenting of my sins, giving my heart to Jesus Christ and receiving Him as my Lord and Savior. I certainly didn't understand it all, but I accepted Christ by faith. I knew in my heart that I had been born again and that my life would be forever changed.

I recall my youth pastor, John McArthur (Dr. John McArthur today) sharing with me the simple acrostic that has stayed with me through my life-FAITH, *Forsaking All I Trust Him.* And that faith became real when it was couples with God's grace. The way I understood it, the picture that made it real and has stayed with me throughout my life has been this. I reached my hand of faith to heaven and God reached his hand to grace-God's riches at Christ's expense. When my faith grasped His grace, the gift of salvation, the transformation of a life, the indwelling of God's precious Holy Spirit and the creation of a new creature in Christ took place.

How did I know this? Well that is where the story began. I knew for certain I was saved in my heart, but this thing called *faith* was like a vast new universe to me, beckoning me to search and seek into its farthest corners each day. I remember my Dad, a project manager with N.A.S.A., talking to me about the never-ending vastness of outer space created by God; and yet that same God loved me enough to die for my sins, care for me each day, and had a wonderful plan for my life.

That fact astounded me and to this very day works wonders in my life!

As time went by, I began to dig into God's Word and follow every text I could to up the wattage on my enlightenment of His gift of faith. Every aspect of my salvation and daily walk with Him was encapsulated in this thing called *faith*. I learned it was so much more than the simple belief or trust system that the world talks about and my friends were building their lives upon. The awesomeness of God, His power in all creation, verified through history, being actualized daily in my young life drove me to a burning desire to know Him more personally, commune with Him continually, and realize His power to direct and make a difference in my life.

Even though I couldn't find an actual definition for faith in the Bible, I discovered something even more wonderful and enlightening. Faith is a gift of God through Jesus Christ that produces daily a confident, unshakeable trust in His faithfulness, and a vibrant expectation of His timely interventions in keeping with His gracious promises to us.

This wonderful faith is a by-product of my personal relationship with Him, and grows from daily knowing and experiencing more of Him! To know Him more was not only my greatest privilege, but was also my greatest need. That was an awesome discovery-the God who had saved me and knew all about me wanted me to know Him! Never in my life was this to be about religion, but instead about a personal relationship.

The five letter word *FAITH* had been at the point of salvation and would continue on a daily basis to be the means to accomplish this wonderful relationship. That is where the road of faith began and now for over 50 years has been an adventure beyond words.

The Faithfulness of God

The faithfulness of God has been ever present. The gentle touch of His hand on my life, the awareness of His love, the joy of

His presence, but most of all, His faithfulness has been astounding. When Christ established in my heart, He began transforming me to be more like Him. As I walked the road and lived my life with Him, He used victories and defeats alike to keep me on the road to spiritual maturity.

I am reminded of the words John Keats wrote in reference to God's faithfulness and the reality of His presence through the years. "Nothing ever becomes real until you have experienced it: even a proverb until your life has illustrated it. Call the world, if you please, the vale of soul-making."

It has been through the vale of difficulties in my life that God has worked and grown me. Truths I professed began to possess me. I had become the convictions that at one time I held theoretically. God has continued to build a bridge between my walk and my talk. I believe as never before that life in Christ is intended to give us depth of personality in which surface beliefs become the fabric of our character. The adventure of obedience to His Word through faith stitches the tapestry, and faith grows! That sounds pretty good, but it is not always easy.

Over the years, a fledging faith has become a beautiful relationship of trust and faithfulness with God. Though I have made so many mistakes in life, He was and is always there. And He will be for you!

One of the sections of that bridge to reality is the glorious fact. *There is nothing I can do to make God love me more; nothing I can do to make him love me less. He, God, simply loves me.* Can I explain that? Not in a million years. But I know it is true! Faith is and has proven it over and over.

Beginning To Learn What Faith Is

In Hebrews, Chapter 11, the Bible tells us that "faith is the assurance of things hoped for, the conviction of things not seen." For by it, the people of old received their commendation that by faith we understand that the universe was created by the Word of God, So that what is seen was not made our of things which are visible. That did not do much to clarify my young faith in Christ. And as I wrestled with that, I found myself continuing and particularly taken by Verse 6, "And without faith it is impossible to please Him, for whoever would draw near to God must believe that He exists, and He rewards those who seek Him."

What was and is encouraging is to realize and remember that Jesus said it takes just a little faith, the faith of a mustard seed, to move mountains. At that point (and on too many occasions today) my faith really seemed pretty small. However, the driving importance of faith kept spurring me on.

God says in Verse 2, that the people of old receive their commendation. I would continually ask myself what that meant to me. It means that He blesses and works in our lives according to our faith. He does not care about my fame, if I amass a fortune, or how great I may look in today's politically correct world. Who my friends are does not Impress God. He is only concerned with my faith. When God measures me and watches me, He's examining my faith. Every time He blesses me or walks me through another "vale of soul-making." He does so according to the hand of faith. As I mentioned earlier, that hand of faith that connected with His hand of grace that brought salvation, is the same hand that reaches out into the unseen world that we read about in Verse 1. "Faith is the assurance of things hoped for, the conviction of things I simply cannot see." That hand of faith brings back the realities of God into my life.

The Bible tells me that the things I desire when I pray, if I believe, I shall have them. The problems I have in my life today, if I really analyze them, are because of my struggle with a lack of faith. How many times in my life have I worried about things that I couldn't understand or control and then through time understood they were there because of my lack of faith.

I believe it is at the point of worry that many other dilemmas and calamities in my life had found a seedbed to grow! For example, the times in my life that I worried and was lonely, the loneliness was again a lack of faith. I realize that Jesus said "I will never leave you or forsake you," but sometimes I didn't trust Him enough to rest on that bridge. Then I realized as I put my faith where it needed to be, that He was there all the time, and it was through my faith that He would make His presence real. Whether it was disobeying what God said to do, whether it was a lack of prayer, or frustration that prayers were not answered-all of them grew out of a lack of faith.

Friends, we know that we get our prayers answered when we pray in faith because all things are possible to him that believes. But this old world has a way of keeping you from living your beliefs. And then like a cold San Francisco night, your faith becomes "fogged in." It can cause you to forget that the blessings of God come through faith and the problems that we so often have come because we simply take our eyes off of Jesus and proceed on our own merit.

I will never forget the example that my friend Dennis Jump (a funny name for a pilot) told me after flying F-4 Phantom jet fighters in Vietnam. He was also familiar with San Francisco fog and said that when flying a fighter at Mach speeds, you flew just like you were in the fog. You only looked at the instrument panel; you did not get your bearings from looking outside the window because sometimes you would not be able to tell if you were upside down or right side up. Vertigo could really ruin your day!

Friend, spiritual vertigo also has a way of fouling up your life bearings. The devil wants us to question what God is doing and not only fog us in, but flip us upside down and around! He may cause you to forget that God's blessings which you have experienced came through faith. You kept your eyes in His Word and on His promises! All we have to do is get alone with God and remember the last time we felt His love and presence, as He massaged our troubled hearts with His blessed assurance! The sweetest times in my life have been spent quietly and peacefully with the Lord and in His Word.

Still, I needed more from my Heavenly Father. Like I said, what is faith? How do I understand it? And how do I recognize God working in my life? It is because I hunger to draw closer to Him.

My quest brought me first of all to try to understand what God expected of me for faith in my daily walk with Him. How could I stay out of the fog? As I stated before, Hebrews 11:1 says, "*faith is the assurance of things hoped for . . .*" I remember glancing at that phrase "hoped for" and wondering again who God really was. Because that phrase says *I'm not complete yet*, I understand that there are things I am going to need; things that God wants me to have. Things I hope for but, in reality, do not have.

I have learned that's not a bad thing, but in actuality a good thing. As I walk with the Lord, I discover that He made me incomplete for a purpose. Each of us has a divine unrest and dissatisfaction. What does that mean to me today? How could this easily-felt reality actually be good and help me grow closer to my Savior?

Perhaps the simplest way for me to grasp this is to think of my favorite dog of years ago-Mr. Dakota. That big old black lab was loved by everyone in the family . . . and by neighbors in every direction! It was so easy to satisfy him if I just gave him certain things. For example, a quiet place, a dog house that was his own, his favorite food, dog biscuits and leftovers when I cooked or went out to eat, a ball to chase, a Frisbee to catch and bring back to me, a pat on the head, or a stroke by his eyes. Then I would have a very happy dog. That's about all it took for old Dakota to be the happiest black lab you could imagine.

As I've watched people through life, I've come to realize that that's about all many of my friends and the world around me were, and are, living for. They go into this politically correct world and what they need is a certain degree, a fancy place to live and sleep, a great sense of achievement, food that they want to eat, and a little affection from this person or that. Is that not really just a dog's life?

And according to what God is saying in His Word, we were made for more than that. The sad this is this. So many people don't even get a dog's life. How many people have you met in stores or wherever you are, that are so unsatisfied and seemingly miserable. You almost think that instead of having a glass of orange juice that morning, they must have swallowed a glass of vinegar by mistake? The sad this is that they are truly miserable and in need of a vibrant faith in the Lord Jesus Christ!

I read that some psychiatrists say Americans today are born crying, live complaining, and die disappointed. They say that youth is a blunder, maturity is a struggle, and old age is regret. Friends, what a horrible picture of life! On the contrary, my youth was a blast. My maturity is an adventure, and my old age is something I forward to-living a legacy in Christ!

However, if you look around today, there are so many people simply living lives of existence and quiet desperation. They are just trying to get by. Like Ernest Hemmingway once said, "We're all ants on a burning log." They are hopeless; they have no assurance in anything.

But God tells me that faith gives me assurance-assurance that I am more than just a creature in this world, and that God loves me for a great reason, a divine destiny. As Zig Ziglar always said, "Through Christ, I've already won."

Faith Gives Substance to Assurance

I have learned that the requirement of faith is this-*we need it to turn our hopes into reality*. If you want to live beyond the dissatisfaction of this world, beyond faded dreams and frustrations that perhaps you've carried through life, then you are required to receive the gift of, and be constantly growing in, God's faith. That faith turns your hopes into reality and keeps you out of the fog. It gives you blessed assurance-the assurance of things hoped for. That faith has been my rock, my lighthouse, and my instrument panel in my deepest times of need.

Having discovered that, I am continually learning that not only is there a requirement and mandatory need for faith in my life, but through Christ I need to understand the essence or heart of faith. What is actually at the core of this incredible gift that God gives us called Faith?

Actually if you go through scripture, God doesn't give a definition like we humans like to have. Remember the old saying: "KISS-Keep it Super Simple?" Well, God didn't do that for me this time. I have unwittingly always sought out an exacting answer to questions of the part or whole of anything that was burning in my mind. Spell it out for me, give me an E=mc2 squared formula.

But it is so much deeper than that. As far as I know, there's not a real definition of faith anywhere in the Bible. But there is a continuing and wonderful description that God gives, especially here in Hebrews 11. I've been watching God turn it into reality for 50+ years in my life. Well, what is the heart of faith? First of all, it says it's the assurance of things hoped for in Verse 1. Secondly, it says it's the conviction of things not seen.

Then notice in Verse 3, that by faith, we understand the things of God. So first of all, faith is assurance. Then it is conviction. And then God gives us understanding.

Understanding was where I began in my walk with and quest for God. Here in Hebrews, I learn that is what faith is. At least that's what faith does. Faith gives me assurance-gives me something I can stand on and trust! Something beneath me is firm and I can put my weight on it without fear.

As I have looked at this verse over the years, I can remember thinking to myself, I can't grasp that. It sounds like a magic show; a computer enhancement that is too quick to understand. What is God saying? I really want something solid.

Friends you'll never find anything more solid than assurance or substance and that's what God tells me faith is. If I will live my life standing by faith on the word of God. It Will bring forth assurance that's solid. It's not a "God's there when you feel good, He's not when you don't" type of thing. Faith has steel in it.

Just like the massive Golden Gate Bridge near where I come from in California. Often you can see the towers of the Golden Gate standing tall and majestic against the clear blue sky high above the dense thick fog on the water below. Clearly seen and solid, it's something that's awesome, something that's huge, and something that seems so indestructible that you can walk right across.

God says faith is assurance. It is something that I have beneath me that is solid because it comes from within me, where the Lord Jesus Christ dwells. Some people say to me, I want reality. Well, you have reality. It may sound kind of redundant, but genuine reality comes when you learn to live by faith. The Bible says faith is the assurance-the solid steel assurance-of things hoped for.

Faith is Evidence

Not only is faith substance, the verse shows me that it is also evidence. At times in my life I remember having reality checks and asking myself-*Is God real? Is the Bible real? How do I really know there is a heaven? How can I really know that Jesus is coming again?* Well, according to this verse, God gives us faith. Faith is the assurance of these things.

Faith doesn't make these. things so. Some people really struggle at this point. They think if you believe, if you pray, if you wish hard enough on anything, it will happen. This was the mentality of my friends when I was first saved at nine years old. Strangely enough, it appears to still be the belief system of a majority of people today. Maybe we bought into Disney when we were little children. You remember when all the little mice would sing "a wish is a dream that comes true" in Cinderella. Or the music and motion picture industry and its influence from "Puff the Magic Dragon" to "Star-Trek.'

Really that's not faith, as wonderful as those stories, songs, and some movies are. When people unwittingly say, "Well, just have faith" . . . that doesn't cut it. If you don't think it will work, just have faith. They don't understand what a Biblical faith is. They think that faith is just positive thinking -mind over matter.

Some people even think faith is optimism-keep a stiff upper lip, be tough, and be macho. If you have the right attitude, you can overcome anything. Maybe they think that faith is just believing that somehow it's all going to work out. Kind of like the ostrich who sticks his head in a hole in the ground and hopes that the thundering herd of water buffalo will see him and go around him.

Faith is not just wishing something so. Things don't come into being because I have faith.

In my life, God has shown me that I have faith because things are already "into being" or "there:' Faith is the assurance of those things, according to that verse. It's the assurance that they're already true.

When I click onto my computer and send an email message to my family hundreds and hundreds of miles away, how do I know that they're there? I get an email sent back to me. How do I know if a computer works? I get a reply. Faith is the assurance of that hope according to the verse. If I simply believe it, that will not hype it up or make it happen. I believe because it is so. It is an assurance God says. My faith is the assurance that is so.

Now you can't have faith for anything that isn't a reality. That is not so. It has to "be so" before you can have faith. So faith according to this verse is rooted in truth from the Word of God. And God gives me a growing faith to show me that those things are true and proves them to me one by one by one!

If this confuses you, as it does me at times, may I invite you to remember what my friend, Zig Ziglar, has said many times to me, "Don't let your worries or questions get the best of you; remember, Moses at one time was a basket case." In my life, I am happy to say that God has always had a grip on the basket and blessed my faithfulness!

As I have followed Him and emblazoned these verses on my heart, it has brought the reality of that song, "Blessed Assurance, Jesus Is Mine:' He would later continually show me that like the old hymn said "Victory in Jesus" was assured if I would keep my eyes on Him and follow in obedience.

Summing it up, faith will bring assurance and happiness to your days. God will give you a hope-saturated joy from His Word and a gentle and solid touch from His presence. Faith will bring a peace and calm to your heart.

Chapter Two

Does Your Faith Make A Difference In Your Life?

The Apostle Paul uses past, present, and future tenses when he talks to us about salvation and faith. In Ephesians 2:8, the Bible says, "For by grace you have been saved through faith . . ." Jesus Christ delivered us from our sins of the cross. As I stated before, this was my wonderful and glorious experience when I prayed to receive Him at nine years old.

When we receive the gift of faith and we commit our lives to Him as Lord and Savior, we are forgiven, as I previously shared. Paul goes on writing to his friends in Corinth and he says, "We are being saved day by day," 1 Corinthians 1:8 Experience by experience; the fresh wonder of belonging to Jesus Christ and the joy and presence of our faith increases.

We will be saved when we have truly been born again! We need have no fear of what will happen to us in the future, in our death or where we will spend eternity. That is what the Apostle Paul shares with the Roman Christians when he writes in Romans 5:9, "Much more than having now been Justified by His blood, we shall be saved from the wrath through Him."

It was wonderful to realize I truly was a new creation in Christ Jesus, a joint heir with Him. The fact that I could not lose that relationship was incredible. You will never find anybody saved twice in the Bible because it never has and never will happen! Salvation is good once and for all when. we. are truly saved. I never received a 10-year or a 25-year life in Jesus.

No, I received "eternal life" in Christ. I remember the old and wise saying, "The faith that fizzles before the finish had a flaw from the first!"

However, in the years that followed, I painfully came to understand that though the relationship would never be changed, I could do things that would really mess up the fellowship.

Dear friend, finding direction for your life in the world that we live in, is not an easy thing to do when you take your eyes off of Jesus. The world tells you that you need to be this -for this person, that-for that person, and the most important thing is that everyone likes you and you are consequently achieving your dreams! Often, God's direction by faith can become so clouded by this world that we lose our direction altogether!

Chasing My Dream

Growing up in Southern California, I soon had my guitar, my singing group, and dreams of being just like Glen Campbell, John Davidson and well, you name him, anyone who was singing for a crowd-pleasing, all-popular, number one recording artist career! As I watched Johnny Carson on television, another voice in me said I wanted to be the next Johnny Carson! Perhaps as you think back over your life, you can remember times when your eyes were off of the Lord, and you had somehow been redirected by the peer-pressure of the world around you.

Being pulled in many directions, I began to think it was not "who I was" but rather "who I knew" that mattered. I soon found myself becoming a chameleon, changing colors and at times changing personalities to try to impress and meet the required need or expectation of the person I was speaking to at any given time. I began viewing people as to their importance in helping me do what I wanted to do, rather than understanding or caring about them as the persons they were!

God's values were no longer my values and His plan for my life definitely was not mine. Faith cannot make a difference in our life unless we place our faith solely in Jesus Christ. He never forces His will upon us. Oh, we may be totally secure in His grip and our salvation, but we can wander a long way away from our Savior, fall into many needless potholes and find ourselves with more "down and discouraged moments" than living in His joy! Can you think back in your life when your goals, opinions and prayers seemed to fall in totally different directions? That you knew in your heart what God's will for you to be?

I can remember putting together a musical group, and as we practiced, sang and made our first 45 rpm record, things began to happen. We became a feature singing group at Disneyland. Our first record was doing well on the radio and charts and we were booked to sing in the Hawaiian Islands with many musical greats like Frankie Laine, Nancy Wilson, Petula Clark and others. It is interesting how important those names and others seemed to be back in those days. However, now they are really meaningless as you think of the scope of what life is in reality and what life is all about!

"National Gallery"
Disneyland
1968

Joe Schofield
Early singing days 1966-70

Friend, have you ever taken time in your life to notice that as you achieve and obtain the things that you have driven so hard for, and think are so important while you are chasing after them? Then once you achieve those goals, they seem so meaningless and empty? That is because they do not touch the deepest points of your heart and they certainly do not supply your need for fulfillment in life. Only one thing never grows old-and that is the love, joy, and the relationship that comes when Jesus Christ is your Savior. Faith will, and does, make a difference when it is centered in Jesus Christ and you are following His directions.

As my mind peruses back to some of the definitive days in my faith walk, I remember when we were singing in the Pacific Ballroom at the Ilekai Hotel and the Golden Anchor Club in Honolulu. Seeing our names up on the giant billboards made me believe that I was really on the road to becoming what I thought was the absolute goal and dream of my life. I enjoyed waking up to read newspaper in those pre-computer days, and the reviews that said we were wonderful and outstanding as a musical group. That I was most surely the "little brother" of John Davidson because of my voice, style and the way I looked. As I think back now, it was all yada, yada, yada and more yada! During that time our group was called back to Los Angeles by our manager, who was one of the heads at NBC Television.

We were to record a new song from Burt Bacharach. I decided I wanted to stay a few more days in Hawaii and see a place called "The Sacred Falls." As I drove my little rented Mustang down the narrow dirt road to the back of a sugar cane field and hiked my way up those fields to a beautiful waterfall, God decided it was time to give me a redirect. I remember sitting down. I was the only one there viewing a large pool of water maybe 100 feet across a volcanic water park, and I heard the Lord's voice very clearly saying to me, "Joe, what are you doing with your life?" Now, at that point, I did not want to hear God's voice. Because in my heart I knew I was not doing what He wanted me to do. I did not know what He desired me to do. But I knew in my spirit that I was doing only what I wanted to do.

Has there been a time in your life when you were running your own agenda? You never did it in a mean or disbelieving fashion, but rather just putting God off for the time being as you discovered your own dreams first.

Wake Up Call

Well, when I heard God's voice speaking to me, I did what I believe we all would do upon hearing from the Lord against our will. I began to argue with God. As I'm thinking back, I can remember saying "God, thank you for saving me and I'm glad I belong to you. "But" . . . and it's usually the "buts" that get us in trouble, isn't it? But dear God, right now I'm sure you've been watching what we're doing. I have been able to sing, and we're recording. I'm writing songs; just look at all the things happening." I won't waste time telling you right now because they are not even impressive to me, and at that time they were totally unimpressive to God. The Bible makes it clear that all the works of our life, whatever we do; they are as filthy rags before God. Our Heavenly Father knows what it cost Him to save us and that was the shed blood of His Son, our Savior, the Lord Jesus Christ.

Well, finding that my arguing with God got me nowhere, I was perplexed. In fact, when we argue with God, I believe He backs up and is once again quiet. And I know He was totally unimpressed with what I had to say. At that point I got quiet again. And that's when, He really appeared. I heard His voice again saying "Joe, you're missing the big picture, son. You're missing in your reality appraisal; you're missing what life and eternity is about. You're missing what I have planned for you and living without the joy that I've paid on the cross for you." I've found in my life that when I hear God and I argue with God and I get quiet and I hear Him again, there is only one thing left for me to do and that is to run.

Perhaps there have been times in your lives, when you've argued with God and it did nothing at all. You decided like me, "I'm going to run from God:' How foolish it is to think that we can go *anywhere* and be somewhere that He is not. I raced back down the pathway, dear friend. I jumped into that little Mustang without opening the door (much like Magnum P.I. used to do in his television shows in those days), and I drove back to the hotel, threw my clothes in my luggage, called the airport saying I needed a ticket not 2 days from now, but right now. Gods in Hawaii and I'm getting out of here.

I can still remember that moment and now I think how stupid that must have sounded to that ticket agent who was on the other end of the line. I raced through the airport, got on the plane and to show you how silly and warped my spiritual values were in those days, I was on my way back to L.A., back to the studios, back to my manager, back with the group, to get back on track with my dreams. I was so far out of touch f om what God wanted me to be doing that my own ignorance filtered down to all areas of my life. That included my financial situation. In those days, at times I would be ready to buy two tickets-one seat for me and one, if necessary, for my guitar.

I would sit by the window and strap my guitar in the seat next to me. I don't even know if that's still legal. But as I strapped my guitar and myself in, I remember feeling that plane's engines begin to go and the whine and the rumble of those big jet engines as the turbines began to spin. I remember sitting with my nose pressed against the window, thinking all will be well In a few hours when I'll be back in Los Angeles and back in my dream.

As the plane began to move forward taxiing to the runway, I felt the throttle and the roar of all the engines on that Boeing 707 as it started meandering down the runway. The meander turned to a gallop and the gallop turned to a run and pretty soon we were speeding down the runway. With my nose still pressed against the glass, I felt my seat lean up and my head lean back as the jet powerfully catapulted off the ground and lifted off into space.

Thinking back at this moment in my life, it's interesting that I got a sense of peace to know that I was off the ground in Hawaii and on my way back to the safety of Hollywood. God loves us so much that sometimes He puts us in awe of who He is in very strange ways. As I looked out my window; the plane quickly climbed circled back around the airport and I could see Honolulu. I could see the yacht harbor, the lagoon between Ilekia and the Hilton Hotels. And I thought to myself, 'Oh, I feel so much better' I knew our name-"The National Gallery"-was on the marquis, and I realized that the hotel room that I just left (where I thought I was such an important person) was looking back at me. The hotel in all its grandeur still impressed me.

But then I realized the plane was climbing and as I looked own, the hotel got smaller and smaller. Pretty so n I could see the lagoon, the Hilton, down Waikiki to the Outrigger, and all the way to the Royal Hawaiian. And as the plane continued to roar upward my nose still pressed against the window, I w ached all of Oahu come into sight and then all of the islands began to take shape as the plane veered westward-Lanai, Kauai, and Oahu. I could see many of the islands and as I stared at them, the realization was starting to come over me of just how insignificant I really was. It seemed like just a few moments later and all I could see below me was the vastness of the ocean, blue and sparkling.

All I could see parallel to me were a few scattered stratus clouds and above me the vastness of the sky. My lips began to tremble and my heart began to pound when I realized that the God of all the ages, who let His Son die on the cross, and whom I had received as my Savior a mere 10½ years earlier was missing me.

Listening and praying for a faith that will follow hard after God . . . from 35,000 feet

But as insignificant as I was, He still loved me. And He was invading my mind and talking to me because I was not in line with the plan He had for my life. Oh, I still loved Him and my faith still believed totally that He was God, but I had forgotten the awesome wonder of who He is! As Zig Ziglar often says, "Many folks want to serve God, But only as advisors." Friend, I had missed the boat, but through His grace, caught the right plane!

I unstrapped my seatbelt and made my way down the long corridor of that 707 to the restroom in the back. I was so moved by the spirit of God, I'd left my guitar which I never did. I slipped into that little room, shut the door, and by then the tears were rolling up into my eyes. I threw water onto my face and looked into that little mirror and realized just how stupid I was-stupid to forget who God was, stupid to be making my own plans, stupid to have been sucked in by the politically correct world, stupid to have thought that I could be everything I needed to everybody so that I could become somebody. And stupid to realize that even if

I became that somebody, how void and meaningless it would be for time and eternity.

Only Jesus can satisfy your soul. It made me think back to Hebrews Chapter 11, as I said in the beginning of this book. I needed to remember what faith was. I had to see again the need for that faith and its nature which said unequivocally that my life should please God. My faith should show it, and there was a necessity that my faith be in the Lord Jesus Christ daily.

That "faith in Him" would only make a difference in my life if *it was the right kind of faith*. As we used to say way back then- tuned-in and turned-on! Getting the message would require some choices to be made.

Chapter Three

So, What Is Really Real?

I am reminded of my first youth pastorate many years ago when. I first arrived in Abilene, Texas and found two young boys holding a string that was projecting far up into the sky and. I couldn't see anything at the end of it. The string seemed to disappear. I said, "what are you doing?" You see, coming from southern California I had no idea what they were up to, nor had I ever seen a string just disappear into space. So, I asked them and they said, "Well Joe, we have a locust and we tied the back legs with a line and we let the locust fly." I remembered the old saying, "The Good Lord didn't create anything without a purpose, but mosquitoes come close!" Now I had discovered red a whole new reason for locusts. The boys told me that it soars high in the sky and it's really up there. I kept looking up to the string until I couldn't see it anymore in the sky. I could not see the locust. So how did I really know it's there?

One of the boys told me that, as the locust moves, he can feel the tug. As it swoops and swerves, the string gives a little jerk in his hand. Friends, faith is that tug you feel in your heart. That quick little movement at times when the Lord says, I'm here. It tells you that the hope is real. It lets you know that the assurance is real. You see, faith is assurance. Faith is conviction. Faith understands.

How many years did I waste as a young man, thinking I was proud to be a pragmatist, or a realist wanting to have a clearer picture of God? Wanting to somehow understand God by pulling him into the realm of what I could touch, hear, or smell, or taste, or see.

The Tug That Teaches!

Time and the world have not changed. The world still thinks with five senses. And, of course, in the politically correct world we find ourselves in today, if it doesn't meet that criteria, it's make-believe. The gentle tug of God on your heart will never be understood apart from a close daily relationship with Him! God had made it clear that things were not as real as I wanted to believe. The things that I could see, touch, taste, hear, and smell always ended up passing away. You know what the Bible says about things that are real and things that are not real? In 2 Corinthians 4:18, the Bible says "*as we look not to the things that are seen, but to the things that are unseen, for the things that are seen are transient, but the things that are unseen are eternal.*"

Now this verse takes me back to the very beginning-the awesomeness and the incredible power of who God is. Think about it. The things that you don't see are eternal, and the things that you do see are passing away. One set is going to last forever. So may I ask you, which one is more real?

I pondered this question in my own heart. What's real and what's going to pass away? Reality would be that which never ends-that doesn't pass away. I could argue with myself that I really want facts, not fiction. But then the more I read God's Word, the greatest fact proven and tested through time is God. And the Bible says "by faith we understand."

Well, all through school, people would say you really can't understand by faith; you have to understand by science. Only ignorance believes by faith in this enlightened world. I would later learn that as Zig Ziglar has often said, "Some minds are like concrete; thoroughly mixed up and permanently set!"

Even my Dad used to say when he laughed at the big bang theory, "Tell me how everything got here, how it all started, and what the elements were that had to be here before the big bang? Where did the stuff come from that exploded?" I can remember my dad sharing and giving testimonies in church with Dr. McArthur. People would say gases solidified. "Well," he would say "what gases? Who put them there? Where did they all come from?"

Then throughout my life I've seen people who've been very intellectual and philosophical about life, and they would tell me there was only one way to explain the way things came into existence. Every time they attempted to explain, the confusion level would continue to rise right off the meter. From years of life, the testimony of my dad and countless others, reading and praying through God's Word and especially watching God, I have learned that by faith *the universe was created by the Word of God so that what is seen was not made out of things that are visible.*

And that's the way it all is. I remember talking with my dad as a boy, saying, "Dad, people just don't believe in anything they can't understand." And he would say the universal response from enlightened Christians, "Well, you tell me how a black cow can eat green grass and produce white milk."

Remember that one? How are you going to understand? The Bible tells me here in the Hebrews 11 that it's *by faith* that we understand. Faith gives us spiritual perception. I came to God *by faith* and I experience God through faith. The requirement of my faith is needed in every aspect of my life. And the heart of faith is that it meets me at the deepest points of my needs. That God not only understands and knows what those needs would be, but has the answer-*by faith*-to meet those needs.

So, the requirement of faith, or to say it another way, the reason I need faith in my life is to turn hope into reality. Life so much more than what this world has to offer. I do not want my mind to be "set" like politically correct, thoroughly mixed-up cement, but rather my heart resting solidly in His hands and plans! Faith is not something that I hype up or ream up or read about to control the circumstances of my life or feel good about myself or better about those around me. No, faith is assurance, faith is conviction, and faith understands.

Faith That Pleases

But, may I go back for a moment to Verse 6 where we began? "Without faith it is impossible to please Him, for whoever would draw near to God must believe that He exists and that He rewards those who seek Him." I need faith in my life and so do you. It's not optional, and it's absolutely the pivotal need of my life to draw me and grow me in my relationship with God which in turn allows me to understand what my life is!

As I stated earlier, to know Him more was not only my greatest privilege, but was my greatest need. If I am to succeed in any aspect of life and if I'm going to please God, then I need ever-growing faith through the Lord Jesus Christ.

My faith will please God and it's totally necessary to remember God's pleasure in my life. When I think of all He has done for me-His faithfulness, His gift of salvation, the wonder of His grace-I have a burning desire to please Him. Why? Because I love Him!

Faith above everything pleases Him. For years I asked myself, "What is it about my faith that pleases my Heavenly Father?" There was a time when I absolutely did not understand that question and honestly, I am still being given insight each day on what that means. I used to believe if God is so wonderful, and I'm sure He is, why doesn't He just prove himself? Then it all came together. If God proved himself to me, then I really wouldn't need faith. Now, think with me for a moment. If he proved himself and I wouldn't need faith and faith pleases God, then I would lose my ability to please God.

Friends, this is what we must see and understand in Verse 6. God doesn't prove himself to me so that I can please Him. It helps me to think of it this way. If God wanted to prove himself to me, He could, any time, any place, and in any way. God could literally split the heavens!

Lying in my bed one morning as a boy, I watched all my books and "stuff" come sliding down and crashing onto my bedroom floor in an earthquake, I realized that I had just seen a mere touch of His power! Perhaps you have driven down a highway and observed a massive thunderstorm as it lit up the entire horizon sending a window-shaking roar as a clap of thunder crashed down from the sky nearby. That was merely a token glimpse of God's power! In fact, I believe that will remind you very quickly that if God is your co-pilot, swap seats!

Yes, if He wanted to get our attention and prove himself, he would have no difficulty in doing that. I remember as a young boy sitting in church when Dr. J. Vernon McGee would be a guest speaker. He would look down at us youngsters in the first few rows and put his hands on each side of the pulpit, lean forward and say, "If God wanted to prove who He was, all He would have to do is lean over and peel back the roof of this church and say 'Boo!' and we 'd believe Him."

I always remember this story because of its power and also because Dr. McGee usually sprayed us in the first couple of rows as he animated and verbalized these powerful statements. I always felt like saying to God, "Yes sir, whatever you want me to do Father. I'll serve you, I'll follow you, I'll be whatever you want me to be in my life and, of course, I'll be faithful." Dr. McGee used to say, "Why doesn't the Lord do it that way?" Friends, if He did, I would no longer have to exercise faith, and He's continually proven it to me throughout these many years because faith is my heartfelt, moral response to Him. It is an "I get to!" It's my faith that pleases Him.

My faith is how I get to respond to the heart of God, and the very nature of God. The older I get, year after year, I've grown to realize that I was made to believe in God, just the way my eye was made to respond to light, or my ears to listen and hear sounds. My heart-your heart-is created to respond to God by faith. That's the way we were lovingly made in His image. If God were to prove himself to me, that would destroy what God really wants from me, because my faith is my heartfelt moral response to God. It comes from deep down in my soul.

In a movie that I saw featuring Clint Eastwood, he had a beautiful Gran Torino. Being an elderly man, he had a granddaughter and a grandson who he really couldn't stand. The granddaughter only treated him nicely because she wanted his Gran Torino when he died-the sooner the better! In the movie as she would play up to him, he had her well figured out. He knew she was just interested in him for what she could get out of him and really didn't love him as a person at all. Sometimes I think my Heavenly Father must feel this way because we seemingly always want God to prove himself, When Christ came into the world, you remember in Matthew 16, they kept saying to Jesus, "You give us a sign, give us a wonder and we'll believe." What they were really saying was, you do something that we can see, hear, taste, touch and smell, and we'll believe who you are.

Later when he was on the cross, they screamed at him, "Come down from the cross and we'll believe you." Jesus made it clear in Matthew 16 when He called them "an evil and adulterous generation seeks for a sign but no sign shall be given to it except the sign of Jonah." In essence, "I'm not here to play games. I'm not here to win American Idol. I'm not here to impress you. I came to pay the price for your sins." Jesus was God. And in the Lord Jesus Christ was all the nature of God himself-fully God, fully man. All the beauty of God, that inner beauty, and the Bible says that open and honest heart and character of her grandfather in Gran Torino, our hearts may be guilty of missing the heart and love of God and who He really is!

Miracles aren't enough when it comes to proof. Do you know why? They aren't enough because even the devil can perform miracles. He's been up to doing that throughout time! Jesus never worked miracles to prove He was the Son of God. His miracles weren't publicity stunts. It always touched my heart as I read in Scripture that when Jesus performed a miracle, he would say "Don't tell anybody."

How different that is from today's world. It is all about me in society and always has been. What's in it for me? If Jesus were here today the crowd would say, "Put that on You Tube. Twitter it quick. Get that around the world on the computer on a website, and get that in the blog." Not my Savior! Jesus said don't tell anybody about that, because it's not a cheap trick. He wasn't trying to get anyone to follow Him by miracles.

Jesus knew what miracles would do. Think with me for a moment. Do you remember the first miracle of turning the water into wine? Later it says many people believed Him when they saw the miracles He did. But the Bible says He himself knew what was in the hearts of those men and He didn't believe them.

Just like Clint Eastwood in Gran Torino, He wasn't fooled for a minute. He knew why they were there. They were sensation seekers, crowd pleasers. When Jesus fed the 5,000, the multitudes gathered all around him. They really loved the loaves and fishes but when He began to speak about the deep reality of the spiritual needs in their lives, then they immediately left Him. Sounds just like so many of the people I can remember from my past that didn't find Jesus interesting enough with their five senses and simply walked away. The Bible says Jesus looked at the disciples and said "will you also leave?" How about you? What would you have done? Better yet, what are you doing with Him in your life and with your faith?

No, I've seen a lot of so-called miracles, but that's not the thing that's allowed my faith to grow and to make me love the Lord more. That's just frosting on the cake. You see, when we say "prove yourself God," if He did prove it, we wouldn't have faith anymore. Faith is the response of my heart to the spirit of God. Just like my eyes respond to light. When I ask myself, *how can I know if there is light?* I simply open my eyes and I see the light. And the beautiful thing is that each and every day as I open my heart to God I realize that He is there.

Once you walk with the Lord, you realize only a fool says in his heart there is no God. When you open your heart He will come in. He will start "tugging" and "teaching." Not only will He come in with His wonderful matchless amazing grace, But He will meet you at the deepest points of your needs and answer the questions of life before you can figure out how to ask them. Faith is assurance, faith is conviction, and faith understands. My faith pleases and honors God. and one of the wonderful things that I continually learn as I have walked with my Savior and continue to grow is that God honors my faith. Without faith, it is impossible to please Him. As one man said to me, "It's an incredibly wonderful Catch 22!"

Tugging, Teaching, Rewarding!

My faith is the vehicle through which God's presence is revealed. That 6th verse again says, ". . . without faith it's impossible to please Him, for whoever would draw near to God must believe that He exists, the He is a rewarded of those who seek Him." How do I know that I'm coming to God? I come by faith. What if I think on a given day I do not have any faith? God gives it to me! God will give it to you. He doesn't as me to supply the faith. I can't dream it up, hype it up, think it up. I can't even make it myself. Faith is that gift of God, through Jesus Christ, that produces daily a confident, unshakeable trust in His faithfulness.

At this point of my life, I've developed a little bit of a lung problem with bronchitis. I've am reminded that I only have two lungs with which to breathe when I forget to watch my schedule and pace. But friend, I know that if God wants me to breathe, he'll allow those lungs to function. If he wants me to believe, then God has to give me the capacity for faith and the object of faith, the Lord Jesus Christ. God always does and always will as it says in Ephesians 2:89, *"for by grace you've been saved through faith and this is not your own doing; it's the gift of God, not a result of works so that no one may boost."*

Not to be redundant, but it is such an exciting fact for eternity. Faith is God's gift to me and to you. He give it to us when our hearts are open. My faith pleases God. Through my faith, He reveals his presence and brings His power to bear in my life.

And without faith, it is impossible to please Him. For whoever would draw near to God must believe He exists, He rewards those who seek Him. He gives power, turns hope into realities, brings dreams to fruition, and gives me a fulfillment that the world can never match or understand. When I need peace, I'm reminded the Bible says, "Thou will keep him in perfect peace; his mind has stayed on thee, because he trusts thee." When I need to overcome this difficult, politically-correct world, I'm reminded this is the victory that overcomes the world, even our faith. When I need my prayers answered in a lone, quiet time with God, I remember what He said, "Whatever things you desire when you pray and believe, you shall have them." And as it says here in Hebrews, "Be it unto you according to your faith, faith releases the power of God."

Though it seems like only yesterday that I was nine years old receiving Christ as my Savior, actually it's been a long and winding road. Through the victories, through the defeats, through the times

I've pleased God, and through the times I've deeply disappointed Him, His faithfulness and His gentle touch through the faith He gave to me will never cease to amaze me. Do I understand what faith is? Well, I am continually learning, according to what God's Word says. But the question comes back to one of the greatest thrills in life which is the understanding that I have so much more learn, experience, and grow through by faith with my Lord Jesus Christ. As Zig Ziglar has been heard today, "God doesn't call the qualified, he qualifies the called!"

The Bible says in Lamentations 3:21-24, "This I recall to mind, therefore I have hope. Through the Lord's mercies we are not consumed, because His compassions fail not. They are new every morning; great is your faithfulness. 'The Lord is my portion,' says my soul, therefore, I hope in Him!"

The Lord Jesus Christ will touch and teach in your life, producing daily a confident, unshakeable, trust in His faithfulness! Through Him, the best is always yet to come. I can't wait to see what the future holds as I live each day by faith! Hey friend, I'm living my legacy; not just leaving it! How about you?

Chapter Four

Choices And Obedience Unleashing A Difference-Making Faith!

Oh yes, I was saved, Oh yes, my life hadn't been terrible, but just as "oh yes," I was completely out of step with Jesus. I thought back to my pastor, Dr. McArthur in one of the messages he preached that there are two kinds of faith. There's the faith of Cain and there's the faith of Abel. The faith of Cain will lead you down the road of your own making and to your own destruction. The faith of Abel will keep you on Jesus.

The Bible tells us in Hebrews 11:1-4 that Abel by faith offered to God a more acceptable, more excellent sacrifice. I remember thinking back to Dr. Jack's message that Abel was a very ordinary man, a sinful man, and yet Abel was listed by God as a great man. Yes, he was looked up to by God and recorded for me to read about today in scripture. Not because he was someone of great ability, but because he was someone with a faith-centered availability, but because he was someone with a faith-centered availability. He listened to God and obeyed, unleashing a difference-making faith into his life! It wasn't who he was, but what he was. It wasn't that he had scholarship, but he had relationship. And I realized again that it's not who you know, but whose you are. My "self-made identify" could never give me satisfaction in life unless it was centered in Jesus Christ, and to do that would require the right choices. My identity would not be in my works of achievements, but my faithfulness and obedience.

I could achieve but rather in my relationship as Colossians 2:9-10 says, "in Christ Jesus." It was and is not my "position" in life, but rather my "possession" of Christ as my Savior that would count for anything in time and eternity! This kind of faith makes a difference. The world was trying to sell me a "faith in me" theology.

We still hear in the world today that all religions, all kinds of faith, they're all the same. We've gone from the new age to the totally self-age. It's all about me, and not about God or anyone else. Cain and Abel make it clear that there are two kinds of faith, which could be equated with two kinds of religion. There's the salvation by works, human effort and merit, a faith in yourself and who you are and what you can do. And then there's a true faith, a true religion, which gives salvation though grave by faith in the shed blood of the Lord Jesus Christ. At that point in my life, I was following and reinventing the faith of Cain rather than growing and honoring my Father in heaven with the faith of Abel.

God gives instructions

Let me show you what I mean. Cain was a tiller of the ground it says in Genesis 4:2. "And again, she bore his brother Abel. Now Abel was a keeper of sheep and Cain was a worker of the ground." That is, he was a farmer, and from all accounts, an incredible farmer. "In the course of time, Cain brought to the Lord an offering of the fruit of the ground."

So I want you to see the faith of Cain because it was unwittingly the faith of Joe Schofield and perhaps it ties closely with where you are in your faith. Cain was a great farmer; nothing wrong with that, but he was a tiller of the ground and God said, "cursed is the ground." Not only is the ground cursed but Cain was a sinner because he was the son of Adam. The Bible said "In Adam, all die". So here's Cain with wicked hands offering to the Lord, the fruit of the cursed land and giving it as an offering. Now it may have been incredibly beautiful. I'm sure it would have been good enough for Harry and David package to be shipped around the world. Probably beautiful vegetables, flowers and such. He was being very faithful he thought; very religious so it would appear. And I think he was probably sincere. Th only problem was as Dr. McArthur used to say, "He was sincere, but he was sincerely wrong." You see, it was faith, a religion of his own imagination, his own ingenuity, his own effort; he was following his dream, with a theology of "me." Cain's eyes were on what he could achieve. His fulfillment was on what he could do and accomplish. The Lord would not accept it because it was a religion or a faith of his own work or self effort.

How many people today have that same kind of faith? Oh, they say they believe in God. They may have even given their life to God and are born-again believers. But by faith in themselves, they are following their own road, setting their own agenda. They believe they are going to please and impress God and, in so doing, have his blessing by their own self effort. They believe in their vulture, their refinement, and their education, but they forgot their faith instead is to be in the Christ of Cavalry alone.

The Bible says Cain's faith was no good. But as you see that verse in Hebrews or you look in the story in Genesis, you also have to lock at Hebrews 9:22. The Bible says, "Woe, they've gone the way of Cain," because it says without the shedding of blood, there is no forgiveness of sin. Cain brought a bloodless sacrifice; something done completely on his own. God would not accept it. Cain brought vegetables. I heard one author say, "You can't get blood out of a turnip."

Well, where did they get this idea? What motivated Cain to bring the vegetables? He got the idea in his own head. He did not get it by divine revelation, but by human ingenuity. His Faith unwittingly, though not turning his back on God, had been placed in his own self effort.

There's great danger here at the point of salvation and a great danger at a fulfilled life with Christ. Have you ever heard anyone say, "I'm going to look for a religion that suits me; a faith that meets my needs?" Or even, "My life doesn't need religion at all; I will be my own god!" Well, you better tell them to stop it, because you need to make sure you have a faith that pleases God. Don't have a faith in a religion or any human idea that comes with ingenuity but rather from divine revelation from God's Word. You can be very religious, but very lost!

You need to make sure you that you've repented of your sins and put your faith in the shed blood of the Lord Jesus Christ at Calvary! Once that's happened, you need to make sure your faith (for it to make a difference) is anchored daily in your communion and relationship with Jesus. You see, if you look at Abel, God had a great respect for his offering and he received it. And what did Abel bring? You remember, He brought an animal. The Bible doesn't say what animal. I believe it was a lamb. He brought the lamb and it was killed with the burnt offering according to God's directions in the Old Testament.

I believe that that represents the shed blood of the Lord Jesus Christ. I believe it's all here with all of my heart and here's why. Abel offered a sacrifice by faith and we must learn this about faith. You cannot have faith unless God first speaks. Faith is your response to the word of God and the will of God (that is faithfulness and obedience).

The Bible says faith comes by hearing and hearing by the word of God. Therefore in order for you to have faith, God has to speak. How could Abel have faith to offer the sacrifice unless God had first said what kind of sacrifice he wanted? God had already told him what kinds of sacrifice. The first gospel sermon had already been preached. It was preached in Genesis 3:15. God told the serpent, "I will put enmity between you and the woman, and between your offspring (the anti-christ) and her offspring (which is Jesus Christ); he shall bruise your head, and you shall bruise his heel."

In other words the seed of the woman is going to bruise the head of the serpent. Jesus Christ is going to crush Satan's head. And Satan is going to wound Jesus Christ. So here is the first gospel sermon ever preached. God gives and illustration in Genesis 3:21. He says, "And the Lord God made for Adam and for his wife garments of skins and clothed them." They'd been trying to hide their shame and nakedness with fig leaves sewn together. You remember the story. It was a clever idea. As intelligent as they were, with great ingenuity they were following their own plans and it must have been rather beautiful. They probably did a good job on it. I wouldn't be surprised if Adam was impressed with the job Eve did sewing them together. Sometimes the things we accomplish may look pretty good at first. That is, until God walks into the midst of the garden and our dreams. It says that they hid themselves. They probably argued with him a little bit but that didn't work and once they heard his voice they just ran. Kind of reminds me of the Sacred Falls in Hawaii.

Does it sound familiar to you? Have there been times in your life that you just up and ran from God because you knew your faith was in what you were doing rather than in what he was trying to do or say. Folks, the faith and religion of man's works can never stand the piercing gaze of the Lord Jesus Christ. He loves you and is watching. Again, what they had done with their own hands wouldn't suffice. God took an innocent animal, shed its blood, and God gave them a covering.

In the Bible, salvation is spoken of as a covering, a robe of righteousness. Innocent blood was shed. Why? Because in Hebrews 9:22 "without the shedding of blood, there is now forgiveness of sin." Cain and Abel knew this. God had already spoken. And that's how by faith Abel gave God the sacrifice that was excellent and accepted.

When we come to the place in our lives where God speaks to our hearts, and we show Him the works of our lives, the accomplishments we have achieved, and it doesn't stand up to the piercing gaze of our precious Savior, *do we realize what that means?*

Yes, we are saved, but we are out of step. Yes, our sins are covered by the shed blood of Calvary, but we need to re-evaluate. Take a long look and begin that look by remembering that it cost God in heaven the shed blood *not just any lamb*, but his precious son Jesus Christ, the sinless one, *not to just cover our sins* but to wash them white as snow. When we look into the awesome loving face of Jesus, and we realize the unfathomable work he did for us at Calvary, as the scripture teaches, anything we've achieved truly is ridiculously small and no better than filthy rags before Him.

The yearning of our heart wants to draw closer to him. *The prayer of our heart is that our faith would be back on line so that it would make a difference. Christ empowered.* The cry of our heart is to turn away from the faith of Cain in what we can do and achieve and run, grabbing the hand of that lead in the direction of pleasing God. We can enjoy the fulfillment, experiencing the excitement, realizing the joy of his acceptance and empowerment to the future he has prepared for us.

Isn't it wonderful that we can look at Romans 3:24 which says, "being justified freely by his grace?" You can't buy it, you don't earn it, you don't deserve it-it's free. Redemption is in Jesus Christ. Jesus is not the best way to heaven; he's the only way to heaven. And following Him daily by faith is not the best way to find fulfillment in this life too. It's the only way. Jesus gives us the peace of knowing like Abel that we are accepted daily as we follow him; that we are looking to him, not leaning to ourselves. The Bible makes it clear in Proverbs; "Trust in the Lord with all your heart. In all your ways acknowledge him and lean not unto your own understanding and he will direct your paths."

That's when the joy comes-*that's when your faith makes the difference*. That's when we don't have a religion, but *we have the reality of a relationship of a loving father in heaven* that walks with us every step of the way every single day! Romans 3:25 says, "Whom God put forward as propitiation by His blood, to be received by faith."

Somebody asked me, what does the word propitiation mean? It means "satisfaction." As I look at my daily life. I can picture it this way. Over here is the holiness of God and over there is the love of God and the mercy of God. And God's holiness on my left must be satisfied and God's righteousness must be satisfied, so the Lord Jesus Christ, the Son of God, left heaven and came to earth, died on the cross and with his royal blood, satisfied all of the Laws demands. And our sins are propitiated, satisfied and paid for through the shed blood of Jesus. Verse 26 says, "It was to show his righteousness at the present time, so that He might be just and the justifier of the one who as faith in Jesus."

Over here he is just; over her he is the justifier. He is the just justifier. Only God can at the same time be righteous and just, and at the same time forgive us of our sins. There is one way and one way only. That is the shed blood of the Lord Jesus Christ! He was obedient to His Father and went to the cross that the scripture might be fulfilled and our faith could have power and meaning. He made the right choices for you and for me.

So it is with our faith. Faith truly is the victory that overcomes the world. As your faith is, so be it unto you. The Bible says when we are saved, our daily walk will be supplied with power, direction, meaning, fulfillment and joy as we experience our daily walk through life with the Savior. As it says in Ephesians 2, faith is finding the footsteps God prepared for us and then simply walking in them.

So the question is, "Do you have the religion of Cain, just any old thing will do and I can do it? I will follow any kind of religion that I want, think about, or think up. Perhaps anything that pleases me is new and different and will make me fit easily and comfortably into a Godbless, politically-correct world? Friend, it will not save you!

It is the religion and faith of Abel that saves. The religion of God's grace, not the religion of man's works. What have you put your faith in for your eternity? The bloodless religion and faith in yourself, or faith in the shed blood of Christ. The Bible says in Hebrews 9:22, "without the shedding of blood there is no remission of sin." The joy of the Christian life comes from walking daily with the Savior. Is my faith the faith of Cain-oh yes I'm saved and I know it, but for now, you just stand over there, God, and for the timebeing let me do what I think I need to do (or at least what the world is telling me to do to succeed). I promise I will check back in later.

One of the most frightening things to me is this. When Christian people reach a certain age, we may unwittingly think that we have seen so much, hear so much, done so much as a Christian that we take our eyes off of God and start doing what we think we should do. We can slip into the faith of Cain, a faith of our own works and merit. Resting on our accomplishments rather than leaning on His promises, again by faith! We may develop a faith in our own works, works which we may feel we understand from years of being a Christian, but works which are out of line because God is not at the center of them. God may have a new plan for a new season of our life.

No sir, I want a daily faith that makes an ever-changing and ever-growing difference in my life. Like Abel, I want a faith that comes from daily obedience and "followership." Whether I agree with what He says to me or not, it makes no difference. I just need to follow Him! I have enough lessons and mistakes in my past to make this a no brainer.

One old saint was hear to have said, "God said it. I believe it. That settles it." I believe that applies with a new and wonderful freshness on a daily basis and throughout the seasons of our lives!

If this strikes you as trite or somewhat meaningless in the new world, maybe you need to get alone with God. Maybe you need to sit on the rocks at the Sacred Falls; maybe you need to look out the window of a 707; or excuse me 747 today. Maybe you need to be totally alone and still (what a totally new concept in today's rush and ready world and society) and let God's voice say once again to you-who He is and whose you are!

Rediscover the awesomeness of what He does, did and will do. You need to hear Him remind you of how much He loves you and all that you mean to Him! After all, He let His Only begotten Son die on that cross just for you. If you were the only person who ever lived, He would have done it for you.

Oh, may we never forget when we sing the beautiful song "Amazing Grace, how sweet the sound that saved a wretch like me," let's remember back when we invited Christ into our hearts and what that meant and felt like to us. Then we may realize when that next verse comes, "When we've been there ten thousand years, bright shining as the sun, we've no less days to sing God's praise than when we first begun." Think of it this way for a moment. Abel has been there thousands of years. Ten million years from now Abel will still be singing and praising the Lord and his righteousness will still be giving a testimony. His faith will still be rewarded.

Dear friend, what I am saying is legitimate faith can, and will, always make a difference-a difference now in our daily life in the fulfillment, peace and joy of walking close with Him. And it will make a difference for eternity! God said, "You are righteous, Abel," and, hallelujah, God says "You are righteous Joe, because of what my Son did for you at Calvary."

I want that to be paramount in my daily faith. You can't just believe in anything. No, you have to believe in the revealed word of God. Then through that faith, He will show you the exciting daily plans for your life! Today and each day, I am not bringing the fruit of the ground, the fruit of my works and ideas from my own ingenuity and selfish desires. Friend, I am claiming the blood of Jesus Christ. In the still quiet moments of the morning, I will continually seek His Face that I may walk the day with Him until I see Him face to face!

Perhaps you would wish to pray a prayer with me like this, "Lord take possession of my thinking, refocus my mind on what you have done for me, inspire my imagination with your vision for me as a healed and a whole person. Thank you for making me not only your own, but one for whom you have planned this very day!"

Chapter Five

Does Your Faith Follow Hard After God?

As long as you live you learn . . .
as long as you learn you live!

After getting things cleared up with my Heavenly Father at 35,000 feet and having seen the awesomeness of who He is while looking out that porthole, I had some serious questions and answers that I needed to ask myself, I had heard it said that faith was walking to the end of your light and stepping into the darkness. And at this point, that phrase meant more to me than I can say. Never again did I want to be stupid enough to follow anyone, anything, or any idea that wasn't directly what God had planned for me. Do you remember times in your life wrestling with God specifically at this point? Only Jesus can satisfy your soul and as you follow Him through life, crawling out a pothole sometimes becomes not only a great spiritual exercise but a great courage and faith builder as well.

So Where Do I Go From Here?

What did God want me to do? How was I to follow Him? What would it mean to walk with Him? So often we hear the figure of speech with the metaphor, "You need to walk with God." What does that mean exactly? Again, Hebrews 11:5 speaks about Enoch, a man who had served God throughout his life, but the 21st verse says that Enoch walked with God. Then again, it's that phrase that we hear today. Are you able to walk with God? Enoch's claim to fame, if you will, is that he walked with God. It was time in my life that I stop looking for fame and fortune and start discovering the joy of simply "walking with God." I believe a better way of saying that today is simply, "How could I have a faith that would follow hard after God?" Why did God save me? Why did God even create me? Often I remember people saying it was so we could serve Him. But I don't believe that's the real reason today. I remember looking out that window at the awesomeness of the clouds and the sky at 35,000 feet and realized that if God wanted servants, His angels could do a far better job than Joe Schofield could. No, God didn't save me primarily to serve Him, but rather to love Him. And He would love me. And it would be that loving relationship that would cause me to have the greatest desire by faith to follow hard after Him each day. The joy of personal intimacy with Him would be a far better light to follow than anything this world could offer.

The Bible says in Micah 6:8 "What des the Lord require of you, but to walk humbly with your God." This would be the faith that would please God. Again, I realized I knew a lot about God, but I was just beginning to know God.

I still remember like it was just yesterday, sitting in the morning worship service with my family at First Southern Baptist church in my hometown, Glendale, California. When Pastor A.J. Kenemer spoke on putting your eyes upon Jesus and following His direction for your life, I realized afresh and anew that was all that mattered.

When the invitation was given, I struggled in my heart with the Lord to go forward and totally with blind faith step out for Him. Faith was still scary and I needed to follow hard after Him. But how? As I said earlier, faith is well spoken of as "walking to the end of your light and stepping into the darkness." After seven verses of "Just as I am," that is just what I did.

A New Horizon

It wasn't long until God led me to leave Southern California and go to Texas. I became a student at Hardin-Simmons University and there God began the next phase of giving me a faith that could follow hard after Him and step into the darkness with Him!

He offered a faith that could walk with Him and understand more of who He is. I'm constantly drawn back to Psalm 37:23-24 where it speaks of this kind of faith and the meaning of walking with God. The 23rd verse says that the steps of a good man are established by the Lord. That's what I wanted in my life.

Arriving at Hardin-Simmons with books in one hand and guitar in the other, I began to meet some wonderful people. It was there I had the privilege of meeting Jack Graham, who's now Dr. Jack Graham, Pastor of Prestonwood Baptist Church in Plano, Texas. He's been my friend for over 40 years. I'm sure I looked a little different arriving on the campus with my jeans, my sandals, and a little (actually quite a bit) longer hair. But the desire of my heart was to somehow learn how to walk with God. I wanted to learn how to serve God, walking with God step by step, one step at a time. The walk of a good man is ordered by the Lord.

The greatest discovery on the face of this earth, other than finding Jesus Christ as your savior, is coming to know God's plan for your life. The greatest achievement is to do it. The only way to accomplish this is having a faith that is willing to follow hard after Him.

In the years ahead, the rest of that verse would become very important to me as I'm sure it has in your life. Steps of a good man are ordered by the Lord and He delights in His way.

"Though he falls, he shall not be utterly cast down, for the Lord will uphold him with His hand." (Psalm 37:23-24) What a great

verse of assurance and what a great impetus to have a faith that follow hard after God.

Arriving at Hardin-Simmons University helped me to realize that I had a lot to learn. There would be a myriad of things to study and many opportunities to grow. With a Bible in one hand and my guitar in the other, I was able to travel to many towns and cities all over West Texas and share in youth revivals and church crusades. You see, many people thought it was really something that I had sung with so many of the musical pop stars of the day, but they didn't know that it meant absolutely nothing without a dynamic relationship with Jesus Christ-and that it meant nothing if it was my idea and not God's plan.

God has a plan for everyone's life. He gave me the blessing of sharing the platform week after week with wonderful friends and committed Christians like Jack Graham (Bible and baseball), Al Staggs (side-splitting humorist), and Paul Hall (know as the Pillsbury doughboy for his laugh), Bill Jackson (man with the heart for missions), and many others. Friends, the desire of my heart was that everyone I spoke and sang to would discover that plan, and follow hard after Him, and that I would better understand it and be in better step with Him.

Finding Those Steps

I think I best understand the "steps of a good man ordered by the Lord," when I think of my kids when they were just learning to walk! Do you remember when your kids were just toddlers and you'd stand them up and they'd put that chubby little hand up and grab hold of your index finger? It was about all they could hold on to and they'd begin to walk and you'd say, "Come on, we can do this," and then their little foot would catch on a pebble and they'd lose the grip on your hand and fall down. It was about that time they'd look up at you with a little bit of fear in their eyes. Then you would reach down and hold their little finger and pull them back up, and holding on to them you would say, "Come on, you can do this. You can walk if you trust me." The next time as she began to fall, she didn't fall. She may sag a little, but she doesn't fall completely. Why is that?

It is because you were holding on to her! That is what the psalmist says when speaking of the steps of a good man.

As I look back to those HSU days and peruse through my life I have to ask myself, "How many times have I stumbled?" Dear friend, how about you? We have all stumbled, but one of the greatest things is to know that God holds onto you. It was during these college years that I learned my security didn't depend on me holding on to God, but instead on His holding on to me! And so it is with you when you belong to Jesus. We are family in Christ. Yes, there were so many times that I felt myself beginning to stumble and fall and God not only grabbed hold of my hand, but literally swept me up in His arms and lovingly held on to me.

As I thought about Enoch pleasing God and walking with the Lord, I became more determined than ever to seek His guidance in my life and His plan for my future. I can still remember on many occasions walking across the quad at HSU and looking up at that beautiful, star-filled Texas sky visualizing my heavenly Father. My mind would go back to the picture of that little child holding his daddy's hand and I would find myself speaking audibly to Him. "Father. I love you. I am thankful that you have brought me here. I am thankful that you are with me here and I ask you to help me please you in all things!"

After all He had done and was doing for me, following hard after Him was paramount in my heart! Realizing it would take a growing faith to please Him (Hebrews 11), I wanted to emulate Enoch throughout my college years and throughout my life. It is faith that pleases God!

Knowing God and Walking with Him?

Now remember, Enoch wasn't just someone who was preached about. No, he was real and so was his faith. He is remembered for that very fact. Each day as I listened to great men of faith teaching me and sharing the experiences with God in their lives, God became more real to me. As you read this page, the question is, "Is He more real to you?"

Dear friend, one of the most important things God taught me in those years was this. You can know God without knowing God. Know all about Him and never experience Him. I watched many people during those years who claimed to know the Savior, but their lives were void of His peace and joy. They did not seem excited in the least to follow hard after God. In fact it seemed they had a lot to say and so little to live. Unlike Enoch, they just did not appear to be walking with God. In fact, I will never forget the Senior Pastor's wife, Sister Margie, comment to me after I had just finished sharing in a youth revival service in her church.

God had moved in the hearts of many students. In fact, I believe nine or ten had made a decision. As I greeted the people leaving the worship center, she waited her turn and then approached me. I saw no smile on her face but rather a scowl. She took me by the tie and said, "Brother Joe, you smiled entirely too much in your message! You gave out a wrong message to the students. When you have been a Christian as long as I have you will realize that your Christianity is a way of life and nothing to be so excited about!" I thought to myself, *now there is a life that I want to emulate which encourages me to walk with God like Enoch!*

Have you ever felt that way in your life? Have you felt like walking with God was seemingly out of the question because someone disillusioned you and you couldn't even find Him at some point? Did you somehow allow someone, something, or the tyranny of your agenda to so fill your daily ledger and schedule that God . . . well, slipped off the radar?

If you can relate, then I must share with you one of God's special plans that evolved from this youth revival 39 years later! While having lunch with three fellow pastors in the Commons at Prestonwood Baptist Church where I am now Associate Pastor for Adult 4 and 5, I felt a tap on my shoulder and turned to see a warm and friendly face. A lovely lady named Keva Green asked me, "Are you Joe Schofield?" To which I kiddingly replied, "that depends if you are from the IRS." She laughed and said, "Yes, you must be Jose Schofield. You still have that sense of humor that I have remembered all these years". It turned out that she was a student (junior in high school) at the youth revival I just mentioned. My friend, Dr. Paul Hall, and I were leading the event and she came forward to give her life to Christ and full-time service. Keva had gone on to Southern Methodist University, received a degree in business, then followed God's call in Perkins School of Theology at SMU. She is now Associate Minster at First Methodist Church in Carrolton Texas, just three blocks or so from our church, Prestonwood Baptist. She had also preached and taught God's Word in England as a missionary for years. She was, and had been, "walking with God" just like Enoch! Knowing God and walking with God; here was a proof from God that He is able. Someone might well say that this special story was just a coincidence. But I know that the old saying Is ever true, "Coincidence is merely when God chooses to remain anonymous!"

Dear friends, the *walking part is the revealing part of what's in your heart*. If you do not walk with God in the everyday ho hum parts of life, perhaps you need to ask yourself if you are walking with Him at all. He wants every moment of your life. When no one is looking or listening!

Enoch is remembered for walking with God at work, at home with his family, everywhere! In thinking back, I remember people saying how much easier it was to walk with God in the past. If I heard it once, I've heard it a thousand times. "Joe, the world is changing for the worst all the time." Years ago it was much easier to walk with the Lord before the corruption of music by the Beatles and rock n' roll, and the total dismemberment of respect in the family and morality society. It is ruining the church. Life was much easier 20-30 years ago and people walked closer to God. We have fallen away from God's Son. Old Enoch must have had it a lot easier than we do today.

Friend, that was in the 1970's and to quote the Virginia Slims ladies cigarette commercial, "We've come a long way baby" since that time, but in a negative direction as far as what God's Word says about society.

Times May Change, but Difficulties Do Not

Think with me for a moment . . . Enoch walked with God when wickedness and lawlessness was actually reaching its climax just the way God said it would. Enoch was "in" the Days of Noah. Those were days much like our days today. The Bible says, "As it was in the days of Noah, so it will be in the coming of the Son of Man."

If Enoch could walk closely with God way back then . . . well, as I discovered in those university days, I too could walk with Him then and today! If I didn't learn to walk with Him in the difficulties of everyday life-in class, in the home, later on the job, with my kids and in every kind of societal change, I wouldn't be able to walk with and please Him in the future. I have realized in retrospect that *if it didn't work then, it wouldn't work now.*

Yes, in school I discovered the busy schedule, tyranny of the agenda, but also the ability by letting Christ Jesus "hold on to my little index finger" of walking with Him!

There was a simple sermon outline in those college days on "problems" that still holds true today. Point #1-I have them. Point #2-you have them. Point #3-we all have them. The point of it all is that nobody is without problems, or as the old Spanish proverb says, "There is no home without its hush." However, if we, like Enoch, will walk with and follow hard after God, the problems will one by one get solved. It will be in God's time for His glory, but they will be lifted.

So How Do I Relate?

I began learning an important life lesson in those years; one that I cam confident can encourage and empower you. Friend, if Enoch could walk with God in that horrible age then I can walk with Him today! Once again I think of what Zig Ziglar has said when we have visited, "God promises a safe landing, not a calm passage!" The Bible says that Enoch maintained his walk with God for 300 years. Now, I am not going to be able to match that achievement, but I have discovered the secret to continue my walk throughout my life and that is the power of God walking beside me and Christ Jesus living inside me. To follow hard after God is not easy. Following hard is a matter of my desire and will. But, in fact, the Christian life is impossible.

There is only one way you can live the Christian life and that is by Christ living His life in you.

To walk with God, to follow hard after God, and to grow in your relationship with Him demands one key element . . . and that is the realization that Christ is living and working in you and through you for His glory and your fulfillment. Just like old Enoch! Sorry, Sister Margie, this realization leads to a life filled with excitement and His joy!

This truth instilled confidence and gave encouragement to me while a student. I still remember this while traveling to sing and share at youth revivals out in West Texas with Jack, AL, or Paul and following miles after miles of giant power lines which weaved their path alongside the highways.

They were, as they are today, way up in the sky and buzzing with power. We would often compare them to the power of God in our lives at HSU. We knew they ended up in giant power plants, and we wondered how all that power was produced. One gentleman, and I cannot remember his name, told us that if we had gone to one of these plants and asked who produced the power, we would have been told "no one!" Those great lines buzzing with power that we seemingly followed forever did not carry anything produced by man, but rather the power was already there in the uranium. It is not produced. It is just released!

Dear friend, that is what the Christian life is-the power is in the indwelling Christ! Therefore, your life ought to be buzzing with anticipation for what He would empower next in your life as you walked with Him. Friend, to follow hard after God doesn't mean you produce that power. No you simply release it by faith. Yes, that same faith which pleases God and leads you as you walk with Him. You just reach your hand up and let Him hold your little finger and you totally trust in Him! (FAITH-Forsaking All I Trust Him). That is the faith that releases His power!

So What Now?

So what did God want me to do? How was I to follow Him? What would it mean to walk with Him? The same as it means today! Maybe you have asked yourself these same questions?

During my university days, I watched my world change around me. I felt my mind stretched and enlightened through what God's Word had to say about that world changing around me. I saw God at work in, and verifying His Word in, the lives of people all around me. But perhaps the greatest thing I learned was that trusting faith was and would forever be the switch that released the dynamo and energy of God's Holy Spirit within me. Life would not be about anyone around me or about me, but only about Him living within me. As I thought of the great men of faith like Enoch and I was blessed to observe some men and women of great faith around me, I prayed in my heart to someday become a man of great faith. Then something beautiful happened. I began to discover the "Peace that passes all understanding" of John 14:27 and started developing the ability to walk with Him!

As Dr. Elwin Skiles, then President of HSU and close friend once told me on one of my evening strolls through quad, "Joe, when it comes to faith and walking with God, the journey of 1,000 miles begins with one step!"

Dear friend, follow hard after God, always remembering in your heart where the power comes from . . . and remind yourself each morning to take on step at a time with His Hand holding mine!

Chapter Six

Faith Tested To Be Unshakeable

Stepping out of my university years was the first step of discovering that following hard after God would be difficult at times. Going from Southwestern Baptist Theological Seminary and then to Golden Gate Seminary in California began to reveal the difference between knowledge and action, talk and walk, acceptance and rejection in a real world.

As I prayed for direction for my wife and me, I was again drawn to Hebrews 11:7 and the way that God revealed the secrets of men of great faith. By faith, Noah being warned by God concerning events as yet unseen, in reverent fear constructed an ark for the saving of his household. By doing this, he condemned the world and became an heir of the righteousness that comes by faith. God was warning Noah of things that were unseen and I was praying to God for insight and direction for the big unseen future I was stepping into.

Faith Reality Check

I was called after months of prayer to be the youth pastor at a fairly large church in California. My wife and I had been earnestly praying for God's next step and we were anxiously anticipating His presence in our new call to serve! When we arrived on a Sunday evening to be presented to the church, I was really shaken and awakened by the events that followed.

Fifteen minutes before the evening service, I was informed by the pastor that the board members just weren't sure about the financial obligation involved in bringing me on staff at that time. They had been discussing me and supposedly praying about our ministry together for about three months, but somehow had now decided that their decision needed to be reversed. We had traveled 300 miles to get there. I had my acceptance sermon ready to go, and truly felt that I was right where God wanted me. It was at this point that events as yet unseen, as we read in Verse 7, became a huge reality and took on a whole new meaning in my life.

Have you ever been in a spot where you've faithfully done everything that God asked you to the best of your knowledge? You were ready to go and then God closed the door? Do you remember the feelings of utter disbelief inside your heart and complete helplessness to do anything? How about what went through your mind as you frantically tried to think of what to say and how to respond? If so, you can understand my feelings. I thought I was ready to go, ready to walk with God, ready to discover what was next on His agenda. But God had another plan. God had more preparation and, much like Noah, God was letting me know there would be floods in my life for which I needed to be prepared.

A few years ago a great movie came out called "Titanic." It weaved a story of romance into a less than romantic story and brought it to life on the big screen. It was the sad and fateful story of the one and only voyage of the Titanic. As famous and awe-inspiring as the Titanic was, it is best remembered for the one this that it did . . . and that was to sink! It had been prepared by shipbuilders to be the only ship made that could never sink. A ship that could take anything the ocean could hand to it, and in its proud opulence sail right on through it!

And looking back at my life, I and many guys I knew coming out of school felt like we were now prepared anything the world had to send to us. We had studied God's Word, we'd worked at His Church, and we were ready to sail! That couples with that youthful spirit that says, "I can't lose; I'm indestructible," made the salvation of the world seem within our grasp! But God knew that He needed to prepare me not to sail on the Titanic in my life, but rather to sail with Him on good ship Grace, through obedience just like Noah did, and trust, beyond what I understood at that point.

You see, the Titanic was marked by confidence. As you know, it was built with water-tight compartments and they said it was unsinkable. Yet, as we know, the only thing it did was sink! It was also marked by a carelessness and superior attitude of the crew sailing and many traveling on board. They weren't paying any attention to the problems, but rather simply enjoying their life in comfort and luxury while floating along toward pending disaster! It was in the midst of this careless attitude that the terrible calamity occurred. At 22 knots, a 300-foot gash was ripped down the side of the ship by an iceberg. The impossible had happened. The Titanic sank!

God Knows What Lies Ahead

God knew that floods would come in my life and He knows that floods will come in your life. Perhaps you are in the midst of a flood at this very moment? As He said to Noah in Verse 7, "by faith he warned him of things that were unseen." And the Bible says that in reverent fear, Noah constructed an ark as God told him for the saving of his household. It says by this he condemned the world and became an heir of righteousness that comes by faith. As I pondered this verse, it became abundantly clear that God did not want me to water down the truth of what His Word said, or to try to relate to a difficult world and be accepted. It also became clear to listen to what certain leaders may be saying and not try to impress them with my responses. That in reverent fear, I must always hear His voice and obey, leaving the results to Him. He knows, He sees and he has my best in mind ad He speaks to me, even when I do not understand and possibly am in a state of hurting temporarily.

My life, and yours, was not to be like the Titanic, made to look really good, but not spiritually seaworthy for the storm that would come in the future. The only sinking- causing inferior steel or rivets would be used when I was not "looking to" and "hearing from" the Master life builder and storm proofer, Jesus Christ my Lord. No, God wanted me like Noah, to build my life like the ark, step by step and prepared by faith. That would produce a future that would be unsinkable. Or in California, unshakeable!

A Trusting and Working Faith

Remember Enoch who walked with God and followed hard after Him? His faith was a walking faith. Now Noah, as he prepared the ark, had a trusting, working faith. It's a beautiful order that God gives us. We worship, then we trust, then we walk, and then we work. All the time God is working His glorious plan through us. The book of James tells us that "faith without works is dead."

As I began to sit up, stand up, and step out, again God reminded me about a trusting, working faith. Yes, I had worshipped the Lord. I was prayerfully striving to walk with Him. Now it was time to work for Him as I allowed Him to work through me. That would involve listening like Noah. Although I did not always understand and sometimes was a quandary, I needed to get to work for Him.

I had said I had faith. I had worked through school and was ready to go, but I had not built that ark that God wanted me to build. If I did not, I would really have no faith. Oh, maybe pride, acceptability, "lookability" (you know the denomination would say I fit the model), but not a maturing-working faith for the next part of the voyage.

How about you? Are you accidentally looking to what you can do, how much you are accepted, or what others may think? Are you mistakenly "working" on what you may think is important to God, but maybe not what He knows is important for you and His plans?

Or maybe you are doing what you think is good, but missing what He is saying is best for you?

As Noah showed his faith by his works, James said you show me your faith without works and I'll show you my faith by my works. The fact that Noah built the ark was concrete evidence of his faith. He obeyed God implicitly! I realize that you don't have faith in God if you simply study the book. You don't really have faith in God if you just think you're worshipping Him. If you go to church, get baptized, go through all the regiments, it may make you feel good. But is God pleased? That doesn't really give you an unshakeable faith. Noah's faith was a working faith totally in touch with God's voice and directions.

Noah's Secret

In Verse 7, Noah's faith was based on God's speaking to him. It says "by faith Noah being warned of God." God had spoken to Noah. Noah didn't just decide to do something on his own.

As I drove back those 300 miles from the church that called and then didn't call me, I heard God's voice speaking loud and clear. Faith isn't positive thinking. It's not what other men may be saying. It is not simply faith in faith, just like it's not faith in yourself or works. It is faith in God. The question would now be, "Would my faith be able to move into the future-unsinkable, unshakeable, and solid in Him?"

The Bible says in Romans that "faith comes by hearing and hearing by the Word of God." So we need to listen to what God is saying, even at the times listening seems to be the most difficult thing to do. The divinely-inspired, supernaturally-preserved Word of God is the basis of our faith and our strength in time of need. On that drive home, I realized that true faith can wait on God. Thinking back to Noah, it was 120 years before the flood came.

Noah waited all this time for the fulfillment of God's promise. I needed to wait on God despite my disappointment, because sometimes faith does not see the fulfillment of God right away. I could truly let my fear mount if I took my eyes off God and forgot about Noah on that dark drive home. To make matters worse, coming over the mountains into Los Angeles, I got stuck in a snow storm and had to stay in a motel, listening to the wind, very cold, and hardly having the money to stay there. I hear God's voice say, "Wait on me, that's what your faith is all about. I will show you where, when, and how to serve me with your life!" I wanted this kind of faith, just like Noah, that could stand alone.

I found myself thinking humanly what would people think, what will they say? How disappointed are they going to be in me. What will the world say? What about those who laughed at me going off to become a pastor? Folks, we live in a godless age where we can't be worried about what other people think. Remember, it's not acceptability or lookability.

Noah lived in an age much like this and stood for God, never wavering. We need to get our eyes off the crowd and keep them in God's Word. Verse 7 says by faith Noah would be warned of things not yet seen is also interesting for another reason. There wasn't any evidence that it had rained to this moment in the world. Nothing in the Bible says it had ever rained. To the contrary, the Bible says that a mist went up and watered the world. So I don't believe there was rain like we know. No rainbow until this time. Most assuredly there had never been a worldwide flood. So Noah didn't say to God, "Now God, you said it's going to rain so put a few clouds up there and a few drops and I'll believe. Oh, and let the other folks see also, so they won't think I am a total nut." No, like we said in the beginning, faith is the evidence of things not seen. The Bible says that Noah had never seen these things. All he had was the plain, straight-up Word of God. God said it and that settled it.

As I sat in the motel room listening to that blizzard, I thought this has never happened to me before. I don't understand why, but faith is the evidence of what God is doing that I cannot see. And it doesn't matter if anyone else sees it or not! Friend, my heart was strengthened as I felt His presence. I was learning what it meant not to walk by sight. Maybe there wasn't a cloud in the sky when God told Noah what to do. And there would be no more tears in my eyes, because I knew that God would come through.

Fear Always Near

In the morning as we prepared to continue the journey home, I couldn't help but have a little fear in my heart as to what to do from this point. And once again, I was drawn to Noah where it says in the Verse 7, he was "moved with fear; he prepared that ark." I felt like I was moving with a little bit of fear, no matter how close I felt to the Lord after the former night of prayer. But there's really nothing wrong with that. When God created us he gave us a self-preservation instinct. The doctor says you need to lose weight or you can have a heart attack. Or the insurance people say you need to be covered in case you have an accident. We do a lot of things because of fear. I remember as a child being told to look both ways before I crossed the road. As my dear mother used to say when it was time to cross the road, "Stop, look, and listen, before you cross the street. Use your eyes, use your ears, and then use your feet." We're motivated by fear every day.

I was fearful now as to what the next step in life would be. But I knew the fear of the Lord was the beginning of wisdom and that trusting in the Lord would bring about the peace of John 14:27. So I decided with the Lord's help not to be motivated by fear, but rather to be empowered by faith.

Dear friend, is there something in your life that has disappointed you, perhaps discouraged you, and is causing you to be more fearful than faithful in your walk with the Lord? Or worse case, have you been so discouraged in life that you refused to turn to the Lord, and fear has just engulfed you? Well, I have good news from God's Word that I pray would lift you up today, even as it did for me many years ago.

From Fear to Fulfillment

My plans had been trashed. My life had been redirected. What did God want me to do? Years earlier I had changed my dreams that involved music and singing. I had redirected my plans and gone to school which involved studying, preaching, and writing. And now the door had been closed on the steps of a church I thought I would minister in. Like Noah, I wanted to have a faith that only walked with God (Enoch), but worked with God! (Noah) A dynamic relationship empowered by God, that was based on what He'd taught me from His Word and was dependent on who He was, not my circumstance. When these things didn't happen, my human side began to react in fear, but I felt so much better in reading that Noah, out of fear, did what God wanted. And the best part of that was that God rewarded his faith. You see, God knew what He was doing and Noah had the foresight to trust in Him.

It was about a week later that I received a telephone call from a man that would become a second father to me. A man that I respect and love to this day and look forward to seeing when I get to heaven. His name was Dr. Clarence Sands, one of the founders of the Conservative Baptist denomination and the Pastor of First Baptist Church of San Jose, California for over 40 years. First Baptist Church of San Jose was known all over the world. It had missionaries on every continent. The ministry of Dr. Clarence Sands had brought countless people to a saving knowledge of Jesus Christ and elevated the message of Christ across the nation and around the world.

I had no idea with my limited foresight what God was doing. Friends, after my disappointing return, I traveled with friends of mine in the singing group, Truth, as they performed concert at First Baptist Church, San Jose, California. It was there that I met Dr. Sands for just a moment at the back of the sanctuary. He came in to check the lighting in the church and I reached out my hand and said, "Hi, I'm Joe Schofield," and he said, "I'm Dr. Clarence Sands. It's nice to meet you". We laughed and shared just a few moments about our love of music and the Lord, and that was it. Little did I know that, that same week I would receive a call from another rather large conservative Baptist church in southern California to come as their youth pastor. I was prayerfully pondering the possibility of that move when Dr. Sands called me. You see, he was with the pastor from this particular church at the Conservative Baptist National Conference in Arizona, when this particular pastor told Dr. Sands that he was thinking about calling this young pastor named Joe Schofield. Dr. Sands told him, "I met him and he seems like a fine young man." Now, here is how God works sometimes when we have no idea. It was at that point, as Dr. Sands later shared with me, that he left the conference room, went back upstairs to his hotel room and called me. In that call, he offered me the position of Minister of Youth for First Baptist Church of San Jose.

When we flew to San Jose and I spent time with Doc and the rest of the staff, there was no question in my mind that God had a great plan for me at that church. It was known as "the church on the hill," "the singing church," and known for its evangelistic heart and music ministry. I'm so glad that God tells us in Hebrews 11:7 that Noah's faith catapulted him beyond his faith and gave him the foresight to understand that God had a wonderful and powerful eternal plan for him.

What's God telling us about faith? He's saying that, like Noah, we should be ready. He said, Joe don't look behind you. Don't let the pain inside cause you to be fearful and possibly miss my plan for you. As it says in Proverbs 3, 5, and 6, we need "to trust in the

Lord with all your heart and lean not to your own understanding. In all your ways, acknowledge Him and He will direct your path."

Are you ready in your life, this very day, for the path He's prepared for you? Are you ready to get off your manmade Titanics and, instead, holding His hand, walk the plank into the good ship Grace and sail with Noah in God's plan that is just for you? Don't let fear lead to failure for a lack of faith. Instead let faith put trust in God's foresight for His faithfulness and your future.

Chapter Seven

Sailing In The Wake Of God's Foresight

God had lifted me by faith through discouragement and despair to the joy of sailing with Him in the voyage He had picked just for me.

When I got to First Baptist Church of San Jose, I began a life-changing ministry with Dr. Clarence Sands. Little did I know that I was about to embark on perhaps the most enjoyable time I had ever had in ministry. You'll remember that I had a dream of singing, playing and arranging music, and I'd put that aside because I felt God's call to go away and study to be in the ministry. Once again God's foresight, just like with Noah, was not only to equip me to build my trust and to grow my faith, but also to bless me with the desire of my heart. Upon beginning our youth ministry at First Baptist Church, I felt God's leading to build the entire ministry and outreach work around a musical theme. And so began a group called "Sonshine." "May the glow of God's Son shine through your life:" Sounds a little cheesy today but it was pretty good stuff in the mid-70s. Parents and Doc Sands loved the name and the kids. Oh, how God blessed!

The Vision

What began with a handful of kids ended up being ministry to hundreds and hundreds of students. We had students representing 33 high schools in the Santa Clara Valley. Sonshine was a "known commodity" on most all those campuses and enjoyed a super reputation! Sonshine evolved by God's grace into a chorale of singers, over 150 strong. A 14-piece, highly selected band came into being. The "Sonshine Band" played at times on their own for many concerts and high school activities in the San Jose area. They were always present to minister as part of Sonshine! We then added the drama troupe comprised of some of the greatest young actors and actresses I had ever known. I still remember the look on Dr. Sands face when the curtains opened in the sanctuary there at First Baptist on a Sunday morning and 200 students with the band and the chorale opened up with the arrangement God allowed me to do on the great hymn, "At the Cross." Its crescendo at the end with a booming brass section ended with a quietly subdued six- part held note. The presence of the Holy Spirit could be felt! The hearts of thousands of people that morning were touched because God was working in the lives of hundreds of high school students.

On many occasions, I would think back to that 11th chapter of Hebrews and think of the road God had taken me down to build my faith to depend upon Him. Now He was giving me the desires of my heart mixed in with the joy of serving Him. Can you think back in your life and remember an incident or series of events through which our loving heavenly Father not only proved His faithfulness to you, but gave you a desire of your heart at the same time? A desire that now was not only something special in your heart, but also something that could be used by Him to impact the lives of others for time and eternity!

Our entire youth ministry revolved around Bible study, credit for Bible Sonshine seminar classes, and preparation for its annual national summer tour, which always began on New Year's Eve. This special youth night culminated in a "praying in" of the New Year and then signing of a Sonshine covenant through which a student would commit his or her life for the next five months, particularly in Bible study, evangelism training and faithfulness to church, in order to qualify going on the summer mission tour with

Sonshine. What a sight that was as literally hundreds of students, many of whom had new and dynamic relationships with the Lord after having been at a Sonshine concert or event that year, would hold hands with their neighbor and pray for the New Year and victory in Jesus!

Each summer, Sonshine traveled over a four-five-week period, usually to 25-30 states and approximately 30 to 35 performances of original Christian musicals that I was able to create and compile with a wonderful staff of interns, parent sponsors, and students. God was so good in that bicentennial year in 1976 that He opened the door for us to take three buses across the nation. The head of the art department at San Jose State University (Mr. Frosty) was a great fan of the group and personally created our logo, designed, and oversaw the painting of our buses. He presented them to us and the church in beautiful red, white and blue colors with stars everywhere formats. The designs were placed on all our records and eight tracks as well as on all our posters and advertising and sent ahead of us across the nation!

With bottles of water and Bibles in their hands, Sonshine traveled across this nation and back each summer sharing its vibrant and living faith in the Lord Jesus Christ!

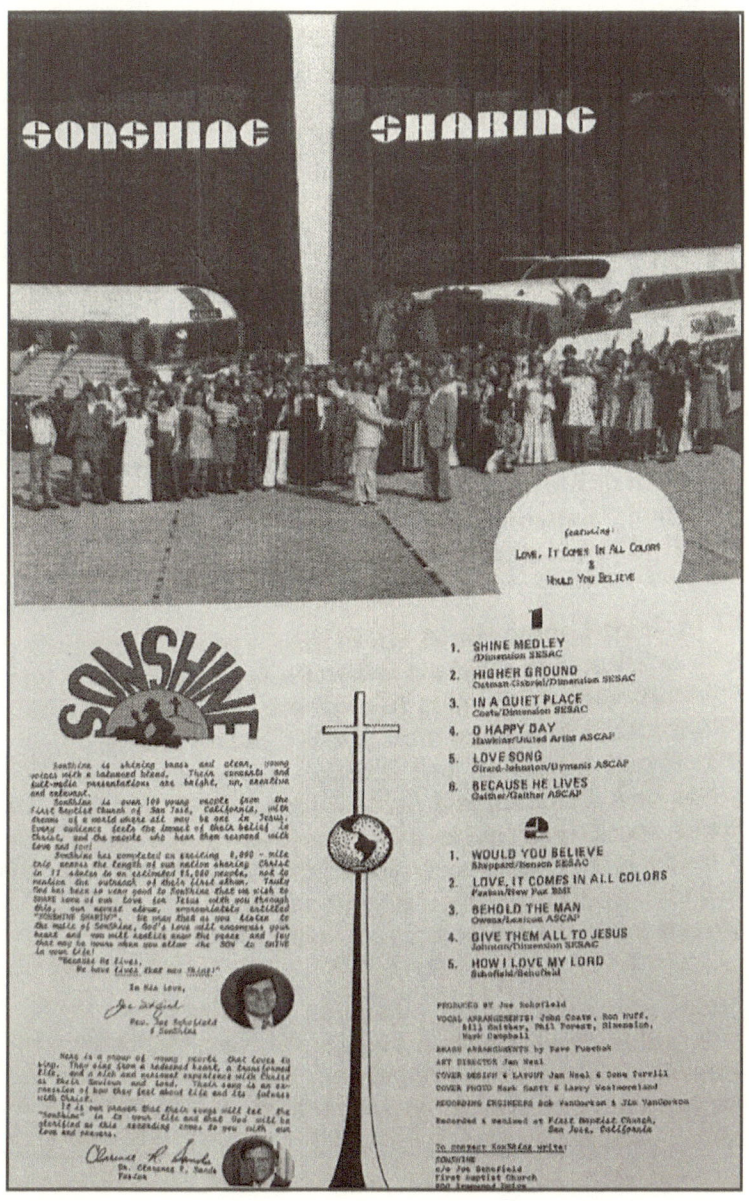

First Baptist Church of San Jose, California
Home of *"Sonshine"*
1974-1978

The Venture

First Baptist Church San Jose and "Sonshine" were on a mission and God was opening doors that we could never have imagined after we began to pray when I first arrived. Dear friend, does this remind you of His gentle and reassuring touch on your life as you peruse back through the corridors of your personal pilgrimage with the Savior? He is always faithful to do and to provide more than we could ever understand because He has a plan and always understands!

On those buses, we travelled for five weeks and watched God work in our midst corporately as well as individually. The beauty was that God not only touched the lives of thousands of people to whom Sonshine sang, witnessed, and shared His Word, but He was also touching and changing the lives of students in Sonshine. I remember so many stories and events. Once in an outdoor concert in Indiana, I watched firsthand the commitment of these wonderful students to reach people for Christ. While singing on choir risers with a smaller version of our "Watch America Program;' I saw girls in the fifth and sixth rows began to waiver and then pass out from the heat. They began falling backwards off the risers. While still singing, the boys quietly stepped down, moved over, and started catching the young ladies as they fell. As quickly as possible, we concluded the song and segwayed into the invitation and sharing of Christ "one on one" time. As I mentally began to realign our witnessing teams to cover the many kids who were getting water and being treated behind the scene, I was very surprised at the coming events.

Our kids did not want to miss their opportunity to witness for Jesus so with water bottles and Bibles in their hands, they made their way to their predetermined spots to share Christ with the scores of students making their way forward. We had over a hundred decisions for Christ that afternoon, which led to a standing room only full concert and drama presentation of "Watch America" at the Civic Center! Not only did the Sonshiners have to overcome physical exhaustion, they had to witness on the spot. Then in a matter of three hours, they had to be ready to begin anew a three-hour program to a packed house; again witnessing to hundreds of students and parents alike. I was deeply moved and actually convicted in my heart.

Have you had moments in your life when God has convicted you about your lack of determination and lack of ability to depend upon His strength when yours was depleted and absolutely missing? Did you doubt that He would come through and in your old nature simply find a way to rationalize your way out of His request? And in so doing, you frankly realized what a blessing He had just for you?

I must share one more experience that God used the kids to remind me He was way ahead of me, just like with Noah! We had just arrived in New Orleans and none of us had ever been there before. As we were seeing a little of the city before getting set up for that evening's performance of "Watch America;' I was reminded of the Chaplain of Bourbon Street, Rev. Bob Harrington's ministry. Some of our students had read and reported from his book on evangelism as part of their study requirements to be on the Sonshine troupe. So, we all headed to Bourbon Street to see Rev. Harrington's work. Well, as you may already know, Bourbon Street in the 70's had an element of ladies of the night advertising their trade from the balconies above the street. Here I was with about 200 high schoolers stretched ahead of me for about two city blocks and they were hearing, seeing and laughing about something they had never been confronted by before. As I clamored to reach my sponsors in person and on walkie-talkies, I was again shown by the Lord that what was alarming me to the tenth degree was a special part of His plan!

The Victory

There was a McDonald's restaurant that filled three store fronts under the aforementioned balconies and our Sonshine leadership had instantly directed the entire entourage single file into the restaurant! As I pushed my way ahead and into the doors, I was again taught a lesson by my Heavenly Father. There stood Sonshine across the entire back and side wall of McDonald's and, when they saw me come in, they counted off the notes and launched into a rousing acapella rendition of out theme song "Since Jesus came into my Heart!" It was the opening cut on our album with sounding brass and drums that was really a fantastic sound! However, I want to tell you that it never sounded as great as it did that moment impromptu, acapella and into the hearts and faces of a very mixed and surprised crowd of people. The management was dumbfounded at first and then taken aback, as was I, at the moving of God's Spirit through that crowd. When the song came to its rousing and full-throttled conclusion, you could have heard a pin drop for about ten seconds. Then suddenly the crowd broke into a wildly cheering, standing ovation. As the tears started to come down my cheeks, I watched Sonshine sing four more songs by request before an unbelievable, cheering audience.

As I began to step up to say "thank you" to the management, our Sonshine officers walked to the counter, thanked the management and slowly turned to the audience. I thought to myself, what will they say?

They simply and powerfully stated that they had just sung about their reason for living-Jesus Christ. They were living by a growing set of principles and beliefs that they had never nor would ever be sorry for choosing! After those words, they thanked the audience of diners and invited them to hear "Watch America" that evening downtown. They then asked if they could have a prayer for everyone present. Yes, they prayed a simple and powerful prayer for God to speak and to reveal Himself and that He be allowed to "change lives" for all who would look to Him! I was so deeply moved by the Holy Spirit that I told the kids later that night before their performance that God had given me a "Life Lesson" on His faithfulness, power and foresight that I would never forget. And He did it through them! I told them how much I loved them and together we loved our wonderful Lord and Savior Jesus Christ.

As you read this, can you remember a life lesson that God has taught you about His power and foresight in your life? Remember whom you were so shaken and didn't know what to do? Then, when you were not looking, He blew you away with simply who He was and what He could do?

Today I still get cards and emails from former students who are now in full-time ministry and whose kids are involved in youth ministries just like we had. During these years, our wonderful children were born-Amy Jo, Courtney Elyse, and John Roger-all of whom are serving the Lord to this day in their lives.

As we joyfully followed the Lord, Sonshine released four albums in the next couple of years. For those of you who may not know what an album is, I've heard it explained this way. It' s a giant black CD that you play on both sides. Trust me, they were something very special in their day. Yes, following God's plan is always an exciting voyage, an incredible trip, and a very high flight. I watched those students share the Lord Jesus Christ from their hearts to thousands of people all across the United States. They shared Christ with no fear. They shared Him with total trust. And it made me think back again to the unsinkable faith of Noah.

The Bible says in Hebrews 11:7 that "by faith Noah being warned by God concerning events as yet unseen in reverent fear constructed an ark for the saving of his household and by this he condemned the world and became an heir of the righteousness that comes by faith." Noah had a message to give and he was no longer moved by fear. I believe he prepared the ark with a "peace" in his heart. God gave him a job to do much like in your life and mine.

I saw that ministry in the face of hundreds of students and countless people. They were giving a forecast much like what Noah was giving. That God had an agenda and He does today. We need to be aware of it and be aligned with it. Noah was kind of a weather forecaster. It reminds me of the old story about the weatherman that had to move from one state to another because the weather didn't agree with him. But Noah had a forecast from God. It is the same one that you and I have to share with the world today. He warned what was going to happen and we shouldn't get the idea that this generation was a generation that did not know. Because the Bible says God spoke to that generation. Noah had been preaching a 120 year-long sermon with nails and a hammer building that ark. And he preached the Word of God exactly as God said it. The Bible says in Genesis 6 that the Spirit of God moved upon those people. It probably was only about 1500 to 1600 years from Adam when the flood came. These people with Noah knew about the Garden of Eden. They knew about Cain and Abel's offerings and what had happened. They knew that Enoch had walked with God and been taken. God had spoken to these people and warned these people. And when you look at that seventh verse, how did Noah know or rather condemn the world? He knew because he forecast that the judgment of God was about to come.

The Need Still the Same

Dear friends, do you want to know what the judgment of this generation is going to be? It's the same judgment that my kids in Sonshine were sharing their testimonies with which to help people. In John 3:19, the Bible says, "And this is the judgment, the light has come into the world, and people love the darkness rather than the light because their deeds were evil." Noah spoke to that generation and they didn't hear: He gave them the forecast from God, but they didn't listen. Does that sound familiar? None of them could say to God, "I didn't know" because the Bible says they did know.

And that once again brings us to the question-is your life in line with God? Have you turned from darkness to light? Have you turned your fears and your failures to faith and foresight by receiving Christ Jesus as your Savior? As I watched those students back then in the 70's and I see them in my mind even now, I know that's the most important question that we can ever answer this side of eternity. But it's interesting that that verse went on to say something else in Verse 7. It says "by faith Noah being warned by God concerning events as yet unseen in reverent fear constructed an ark for the saving of his household but by this he condemned the world and became an heir of the righteousness by faith."

There's that wonderful word faith again. Noah got an inheritance. He gained an incredible fortune. An heir of righteousness, it says, by his faith. Not only that, have you thought about how much time and energy he put into that ark? It has to be mind boggling! Do you ever wonder what it would have taken to build a ship that big-120 years in the making? I mean the Bible says in the days of Noah there were people all around him, marrying, living their lives on the wild side. They probably thought he was a fool. Yes, they must have believed that old Noah was definitely a religious fanatic! They were investing in real estate, stocks and bonds. Probably much the same thing as we do today. Noah didn't have those things. Noah was "Depression Proof!" But the turning point came according to scripture when their socalled real estate wasn't very real because it was covered with water. They lost it all. But when you look at Noah in this verse, he didn't lose it. He gained it. Because later when that boat landed, he stepped off the boat into a whole new world. He owned it all! The Bible says, "Blessed are the meek, for they shall inherit the earth."

Our Sonshine Chorale used to sing a song called "The Meek Shall Inherit the Earth." They began to see in their young lives that having faith in God's foresight and plan for their lives was more important than trying to figure it out. Even in the 70's when I don't remember hearing the term "politically correct," the world still tried to stretch you in every direction other than listening to God. After all, only people who have committed intellectual suicide would seek something called God for life direction! However, the Bible has made it clear in my life and in the lives of those kids that I had the privilege of working with that what God gives you in this life cannot be matched by anything in the world. And that you can't out-give God because He just keeps giving and blessing and growing you as you faithfully follow Him. The Bible says Noah became an heir of righteousness. He inherited it by faith. And as we used to say in Sonshine, "Lord, help people to know they need to be righteous today." The only way one can be made righteous is not by works, not by keeping the commandments, not by being politically correct, not even by having the greatest band, the greatest album, or the greatest achievements. It comes by trusting in the Lord Jesus Christ.

Noah's faith which incredibly followed his earlier fear has always been a source of great encouragement to me. I am reminded of this when I look over my shoulder or into the future. And I trust you will too. It also teaches us a wonderful eternal lesson. You see, his faith was a picture of our faith in the Lord Jesus Christ. And that's the reason the ark only had one door. Jesus said, "I am the way, the truth and the light; no man comes to the father but by me." Jesus said, "I am the door, by me you may enter and you shall be saved." Now, that gangplank or entrance was faith and we come to that ark by faith. The Bible says in Genesis 7 that when Noah went in the ark, God shut that door. God said, "Come into the ark:' This tells me that God was already in the ark. When Noah went in, there was God! He was safe with God. The Bible tells us in Ephesians that after we believe, we are sealed with the Holy Spirit of promise. We are secure in the Lord Jesus Christ.

His Assurance Always Came

I remember going from fear and disappointment, discouragement from the debacle in the lost call of that church to a fresh realization of how secure I was in the grip of God's grace. That realization becomes fresher with each passing year! How my life had been planned out by God before the foundation of the world and my job was simply to follow in the steps that He had prepared. And more than that I learned, like Noah, the best foresight we can have is the realization of the fact that God is in control. We're sealed in Christ.

Thinking back to all those students in those wonderful times in ministry, I remember Dr. Sands flying all the way back with his wife, Loretta, to meet us in Washington, D.C. as we sang with our Senator, Mr. Norm Maneta, on the steps of the Capitol, back in a time when there were no terrorist threats. I was tired. It had been a long three weeks and as we prepared to sing, I turned when the limo drove up with Dr. Sands and Loretta! When they got out, Doc walked over and gave me a big hug. He looked at me and said, "I know God has been with you and Sonshine every step of the way and He will now speak through all of you this very day." God gave me a visual picture of a wonderful "eternal truth" through Doc. I wanted to spend the rest of my life in ministry, serving and sailing on the good ship, Grace, in the center of God's will!

When I thought of all the difficulties we'd had on that trip, inclusive of one of our boys actually accidentally sinking a pastor's boat that was moored at his lake house in Indiana, I was reminded of that ark. You see, Noah probably fell down many times inside that ark during his trip, but he never fell out of the ark. He was in the ark and God had shut the door and all the storms and the waves and the water had battered the ark. It was Christ who took our judgment. We are in His arms and safe. In Christ, we're secure, satisfied, and we, like Noah, are made righteous. Is that where you find yourself today? At this very moment? Friend, that is where you can be.

Also remember that being in Christ, we are given a fulfillment, a purpose, and a power in life, which this politically-correct society can never begin to understand, let alone begin to endow upon people's lives. Verse 7 says Noah was given a fortune. He became an heir of righteousness. I know in my heart, and I pray you know today, that we not only have our sins forgiven, but God gives us a new heart! He gives us a fulfilling life, and he gives us the "peace that passes understanding" that comes from the joy of His presence. There are no words that can express that!

That joy is always fresh in my heart, when I think of Doc Sands, when I think of all of the students in Sonshine, and when I think of the look on the faces of people that they ministered to. I'm thankful that like Noah, I am an heir of righteousness, with my sins forgiven and my life in God's hands. Dear friend, is your faith unshakeable? Unsinkable? And is your life anchored in a personal relationship with Jesus Christ? Are your sins forgiven and under His blood? And when He comes again, will you be ready to meet Him? Sorry that is a lot of questions. But praise God, I know I have the answers and so may you!

If all that's true and you have the answers too, then is there somebody somewhere right now who's thinking about you because you, like Dr. Sands have been a visible proof of an invisible Christ by the way you have encouraged and loved them?

When Doc preached, in his message he would often stop, raise his right hand and forefinger to his mouth and say "Shh! Shh! Listen now, as I want to be understood!"

Dear friends, shh! shh! I am praying this moment (and I believe that Noah is too) that you are prayerfully understanding what God is saying to and for you.

Chapter Eight

We Know He Is There!

"God can't work through you, until He works in you . . . God works from the inside out!"
James 3:1

As I continued down the road of life as we all do, I came upon new vistas and valleys of ministry and discouragement, all used by God for His purpose. After ministries in Arizona and Georgia, working with collegiate and high school students, I accepted a call to become only the second Pastor to Single Adults at Neighborhood Church, a large church in the San Francisco Bay Area. We started as a very small ministry with only 22 people. But very soon as God blessed, we grew well into the hundreds, comprised of single adults seeking by faith the way to put their life back in line with God's purpose. They were trying to once again discern the difference between belief and unbelief, between finite and infinite, between feeling like a lowly worm and being a joint heir of Christ with Almighty God as their loving father. They were searching for His purpose and a powerful faith.

He Completes Us

We decided to use the name "The Single Purpose" which we tied with Colossians 2:9-10 which says we are complete in Christ who's the head of all power and principality. We wanted to make it clear that the purpose in life was not being single or married. It was to be in the center of God's Will, understanding Hid call for you. I would tell them, according to God's Word, it is not my position in life, but my possession in Christ. So "The Single Purpose" was launched and, before it was done, hundreds of single adults were not only finding His purpose, but were also ministering through His power to singles all over the Bay area.

They had put together and published their own paper called "The Single Purpose" which was requested by singles in eight different states. Personally, I kept asking God to help me to give them needs-meeting answers. Help me to be a visible proof of who you are to them, much like Dr. Sands had been to me. I really believed that, even though we know that Christ Jesus died on the cross for our sins, we are forgiven, that He is with us, and that He is coming again for us. As human beings, we sometimes need more.

He Gives Us One Another

The best example of this, as I thought of those precious single lives, was given to me by my son, John Roger, who was about three years-old at the time. We lived in a house on the side of a hill with the top floors being the bedrooms, the middle floor being the living area, and the bottom floor being the kitchen and my study. One night a thunderstorm hit. The sky was lighting up, the wind was blowing, and the thunder was roaring. As the clasps of sound vibrated through our house, my son, John, would yell for me. I remember running up one, two, three flights of stairs. Turning down the hallway, I could see him kneeling on his little bed, a bunk bed in which he inhabited the top bunk. The bottom bunk was filled with his teddy bears and stuffed 49ers. I went close and gave him a hug and, as he put his little arms around me and pulled my head close, he said, "Daddy, I'm scared." I said, "John, it's ok. Remember, Daddy's downstairs and Jesus is here with you." He said, "I know Daddy." I gave him a hug, tucked him in, and went back down three flights of stairs to my study. By that time another big clap of lightning hit, the thundered roared and he screamed again, "Daddy!" It was back up three flights of stairs. For time's sake, I'll tell you that on the fourth time as I made my way back up the stairs, the human side took over more than the spiritual side and the man in me said, "I've got to make him a little man:' And as I turned the corner, I looked a little more sternly this time. Walking down the hall before I got there, he kneeled up again on the top bunk, held his arms out to me and as I drew close, with tears he said, "Daddy, Daddy, I know Jesus is here, but I need to see someone with some skin:' I've never forgotten that. So often I've said to people, from students I've taught to people as a pastor, "Everyone's life ought to be better for having crossed your path during the day. Through Christ, give them a little lift;' You ask Him to help you flesh out who He is to someone who needs to feel and see Jesus.

Having said that, "The Single Purpose" was a very difficult ministry in many ways, but it became perhaps the most loving and rewarding of all my years as a pastor.

Our singles were in three divisions once we got going. They went anywhere from 20 to 30 and from 30 to 50, and 50 right on to going home. But the majority of them all had a pale of hopelessness that seemed to hang over them. They had false hopes that had been exposed as unreliable and inadequate in their lives. And they, as Christians, had gone into their closets, not to pray, but to hide from life. They had little time or energy to share their life with others because they'd felt so beaten back through their problems.

Many had gone through the sting of a divorce, the trauma of the loss of a spouse, and some just feeling like they were half a person because they were single and incredibly lonely. How often did I hear that they wanted to find someone to be married to and how often I would say, according to Colossians, you're not half a person looking for another half to link up and make a whole, but rather you are complete in Christ and when God's plan comes to fruition, it'll be two complete lives together stepping into God's will and pilgrimage for your lives. I remember seeing a picture painted by G. F. Watts of a blindfolded woman with her head bowed and holding a lyre, sitting on a sphere which we suppose is the world. Only one string of the instrument remains unbroken, only one star shines in the dark sky. In an effort to interpret his painting for those who might not catch its symbolic meaning, the artist had a one-word sign placed beneath the painting when it was hung in an art gallery. The word was Hope. The art gallery was in England. The story goes that one evening, two cockney cleaning women stood looking at the painting. One, somewhat mystified, wondered, hope. "Now why would that be called hope?" Well, the other cleaning woman said, "I suppose she's hoping she ain't going to fall off."

So many of our singles seem to share that same feeling stated by the maid, as they struggled to find their single purpose with God! The one string we have left that we think is hope is frayed and about to break. And we're afraid the world that we are sitting on so insecurely has run wild and is out of orbit. We don't know what to do and we've come to the frightening conclusion that hope-based on the inept goodness of people, the politically correct values we've tried to facilitate in our lives, the ability to solve our own problems-is ill-founded and just isn't going to work. These problems don't just pertain to single adults but at that time they were devastating the lives of our people.

God Always Gives Hope and a Plan

Once again I went back to Hebrews to see what God's Word had to say about faith in the midst of difficult times. That great faith chapter spoke about Abel, and reminded me of what worshipping faith did. I mean, Enoch wanting to walk with God and Noah and the stability of his faith that was working. I found myself saying, "Lord, help me to understand what I am to be and what I am to say to be your minister in these lives." The Bible says according to your faith, be it unto you, and it also says "without faith, it is impossible to please God." It's at this point of Verse 8 that God spoke to my heart and I can tell you, encouraged countless single adults as they got their lives, reunited, empowered by, in love with, and serving the Lord Jesus Christ. Verse 8 says, "By faith Abraham obeyed when he was called to go out to a place where he was to receive an inheritance. Not knowing where he was going and he went out." By faith he went to live in a land of promise as in a foreign land living in tents with Isaac and Jacob, heirs with him of the same purpose.

Now when you study Abraham, you find someone you can really relate to. Abraham had things that were good about him and some things that weren't quite so good. He was a transparent man, and singles were really able to relate to him. Abraham was not a perfect man. He had a lot of failures in his life. And sometimes the singles would say, "Pastor Joe, as I study the Bible and most of these guys had their acts together, things were always good. But if you look at old father Abraham, you find out he was a man marked by imperfection." As I shared with the singles, he was a man known to consistently experience failure.

When you read about him in Hebrews 11:8, you discover there's not even a hint of failure. You'd think Abraham never made a mistake. And I shared with those single adults, no matter what mistakes you've made in your life, you need to end up on this side of error by bridging it with your relationship with Christ. In Genesis 12, the Lord told Abraham to get out of the country and get out of his father's house and go to a land that He would show him. God said this to Abram because that was his name back then. Now actually if you'll read it, Abraham didn't do so well in the obedience. He didn't obey God and go where he was directed. He wasn't dependent on God. He came up with his own answers when there was a famine in the land. He decided how to take care of it himself. No one told him to go to Egypt. He made up his own mind. He was working with reason rather than revelation.

This is precisely where many of the single adults shared with me they had found their lives. The world teaches us to make our decisions, to get an education, to stay ahead of the pack, and be leaders in what we do. God teaches us to look to Him by faith in everything we do. Either you're going to walk by faith and revelation or you're going to walk by sight and reason. You're going to walk by trusting and listening to God or by seeing and thinking your own way in this world. Reason and faith are like two sides of an hour glass. One side is full; the other side is empty. When you turn it over, the bottom part gets full, and the top part becomes empty. One side is reason, the other side is revelation. One side is faith, the other side is sight. You have to walk by one or the other. Abraham didn't do that. We don't do that sometimes. It's kind of like he trusted God to get him from Ur to Canaan, but he couldn't trust God once he got there. And that's the way many of our people were with their testimonies and perhaps you can also relate today. We trusted God to a certain point in our life, but then on certain decisions we made them on our own. We trust God to save us, but sometimes we don't trust Him to feed us. We trust God with our souls, but sometimes we can't trust Him with our money. We trust for eternity, but we don't really trust Him for this very week.

Listening to Him . . . or to Man?

Abraham gave a great picture of where many of those single adults were and where we can find ourselves if we're not careful. We discover a lack of obedience, a lack of dependence, and even a lack of honesty with God. In fact, it says in Genesis 12:11 that Abraham was afraid to enter Egypt because of how beautiful his wife, Sara, was. Verse 12 says "It will come to pass that when the Egyptians see her, they shall say this is his wife and they will kill me. And they will save your lives. Say, I pray, you are my sister that it will be will with me for your sake, and my soul will live because of you. Basically, he said "We're going to lie about it. He was going to deny that Sara was his wife to save his own skin. So, when you really look at Abraham, as I used to tell our singles, I can't see why he's such a wonderful person. Why is he so revered in this

11th Chapter of Hebrews? He hadn't done too many things right. Perhaps he himself, if alive at that time, could have been in our Single Purpose ministry. But here's the best part. Hebrews is the way God summed up Abraham's life. When God came to write the bottom line on his life, you know what God remembered? He didn't remember his faults nor his failures, but only his faith. Abraham was certainly not perfect. And Abraham was not always as patient as he needed to be.

Patience was a key word in the lives of our adult ministry and continues to be in our lives to this day! Many times there were discussions and seminars and special services on patience in how to find the right person for your life and being prepared for marriage. Many times singles would say, "Joe, we want so much to have a family and children." Abraham would have fit right in. In Genesis 15:3-6, another great episode of God working in the patience of his choice servant. Just the way God works on the patience in you and in me. Abraham said basically, "Lord. I don't have a son, I don't have an heir, and what am I going to do?" But when you get to the bottom of The story in Verse 6, it says, "and he believed in the Lord and He counted it to him for righteousness." Now you know how Abraham was justified? He was justified by faith. The Bible tells us today that God counted it for him to righteousness. This is how Abraham became righteous. It certainly wasn't his impatient, Impetuous side. He became righteous, not by good deeds or good works, but by trusting God.

Now, there is no better message that could have been given to single adults who were striving to find their lives in the center of God's will, looking for that single purpose, than to understand and trust God. And again Abraham, being just a man, when you look at Genesis 16: 1, kind of messed up the whole situation. He made his own plan. His trust ran out and he decided to just have a child by proxy. You know the story. Sara, Abraham's wife took Hagar, the handmaid and servant, after they dwelled 12 years in the land of Canaan, and gave her to her husband, Abraham, to be his wife.

Now what happened here was that Abraham had an illicit affair with his wife's handmaiden and her name was Hagar. A son was born and his name was Ishmael. He was not the son of promise. He was not God's plan. He was not God's way. But here was the situation caused by an impatient man.

Dear friends, you can't help but wonder how much of the turmoil and tragedy we have today in the Middle East and the whole world with Islamic Jihad and terrorism may be a direct result of this impatient man, Abraham, who failed to wait on God. Single Purpose folks needed to learn the same thing we need to learn and know today. When God says He's going to do something, He's going to do it. The Bible says the Lord is not slack concerning His promise. When God says it, that settles it.

One of the things I continue to learn in life is that God is never in a hurry. I'm sure that you can look back in your life and realize He's never been early, but He's never been late. It's the same when our Savior came into the world. The Bible says, "in the fullness of time God sent forth His son." And folks, do you know when Jesus is coming again? Well, when God's ready. No sooner or no later. The Bible speaks about the "last days and the promise of His coming." Everything is going to continue just the way it is and has been from the beginning. Maybe so, but God will come when He's ready.

I shared with our Single Purpose people about the answers to their prayers. God will answer when He's ready. Don't be impatient. Don't let the world make you imperfect. Just keep trusting and the Lord will take care of this. We do need to know this. Faith has a trust element to it. And it also has a time element. Abraham believed in the trust elements. He just didn't get the time element straight. It says that the believing part was counted onto him for righteousness, but then he became kind of an unbelieving believer. He would have really fit into the Single Purpose ministry at that point. So many folks took things into their own hands and really botched up their lives. Abraham did the same. It takes faith and it takes patience.

In Hebrews 6:12, the Bible says, "so that you may not be sluggish, but initiators of those who through faith and patience, inherit the promises." It's dangerous to be impatient when God has such a glorious plan-Psalm 37:3, "trust in the Lord," and Psalm 37:7, "rest in the Lord and wait patiently for Him."

It was difficult in those years to share with single adults that they needed not to be restless, but to wait on what God was doing. God was, and is, always faithful.

Abraham was remembered in Hebrews because of his great faith. His great faith made him a man who made the greatest impression on mankind. If you think of it, today the Jews reverence Abraham, Christians reverence Abraham, and Moslems reverence Abraham. They all look to him. He was impressive. And what made him impressive was his faithfulness.

We used to talk in the singles meetings and I would say, "If the Lord says 'go,' we'd probably say, 'OK Lord, where are we going?'" And if God said, "I'm not telling you the answer yet, stand up and let's go!" Would we follow Him? If He said, "I've got a plan for your life. Just go out that door and leave your family and everything and trust me." None of us could honestly say we could do that. That's where Christ Jesus comes in. We talked about Abraham, but we felt the presence of Jesus Christ. We discussed how we could follow God because of the indwelling of His Holy Spirit. And that the Single Purpose for our life could become a fulfilling reality when we did walk out that door and accept all that Christ said by faith. We needed to stop dabbling with what the world was saying and being so concerned with what other people thought. But be totally sold out to what our Heavenly Father was saying!

His Message Right Before Our Eyes

I was reminded one night after a Single Purpose service, that I had built a t-bar swing set for Amy Jo, Courtney, and JR, my son. It was a T-bar that went up about 10 feet and crossed over with three swings and a slide under it. I remember I didn't know much about putting in swings, so I had put a 100-lb bag of cement on each of the bases of the poles holding up the swing. I was later told that one bag would have covered the entire swing, but I used 100 lbs. on every leg of the swing. I'm confident to this day that, if the great earthquake ever hits the bay area and if there's anything left standing, it will be that swing set However; be that as it may, one night Amy slipped out to the backyard and went out to swing, but it got dark.

And she called out to me, "Daddy." When I went outside, she was on the top which was a crossbar ladder, and she was frozen and afraid. She couldn't move. And wouldn't you know, I flipped the back spotlight on the backyard and it went out just at that moment. I still remember Amy Jo's little sister and brother, Courtney and John, standing in the door. With fear in their eyes, they were hollering to their sister in the dark "Don't move, Amy Jo. Don't move!" Amy Jo was always the daredevil of my kids, but this time she had gotten herself in a "proverbial pickle" and her little sister and brother were very concerned about her situation. You see, Courtney was the "calm one" and John Roger was the "let's wait and see one." So together, they kept a pretty good "checks and balance" system going most of the time! As I think back, this seemed to happen quite often as I watched our precious kids grow up together!

So I walked out there in the dark, and she could kind of see me, but not very well because it was really dark that night. And she looked down and said, "Daddy, I'm afraid." I said, "It's OK, Amy Jo. I'm right here." And she said, "I can't get down." I said, "Well honey, remember the ladder part of your swing is just over to your right. You just go about four rungs over and you can crawl down the ladder." She looked in that direction and looked back in my direction and said, "Daddy, I'm scared."

At that point, I walked right up underneath the ladder and it was so dark. And even though, her eyes had gotten accustomed to the dark, she kept saying she couldn't see me very well. I said, "Amy, I'm right here." She said, "But Daddy, you seem so far away." I said, "That's alright, I can see you. Just jump, and I'll catch you." And she said, "Daddy, I'm afraid." I thought, "What'll I say now Lord?" I looked up and said, "Honey, do you believe that I'm right here?" And she said, "Well yeah, Daddy, because I can hear you and I'm talking to you." "OK," I said, "Sweetie, do you think Daddy's strong enough to catch you?" And she said, "I know you are Daddy. You can catch Me." I said, "OK, do you believe that I love you?" She said, "Daddy, I know you love me." At this point, her little brother and sister had run outside too and were standing on each side of me in the dark. And I said, "Alright, have I ever told you a lie?" And she said, "No, Daddy." I said, "Then, Amy Jo, I'm here. You know I love you. You know I'm strong enough to catch you. I've never told you a lie. Jump sweetie." She said, "OK, Daddy, here I come." At that point she let go and just jumped right at me. And as I caught her and gave her a big hug, with tears in her eyes, she gave me a hug I will never forget. Even Courtney and J.R. were jumping up and down cheering!

That week in our Single Purpose worship service (after sharing this story), I said, "Folks, that's exactly what faith is. That's exactly what your single purpose in life is in trusting the Lord." The Bible says, "Who we have not seen, we love." And we know He's there. We know Jesus died on the cross for our sins. We hear Him speak to us. We know that He cannot lie. We know His strength. We've felt His provision in our life. We definitely have felt His love. When He says, "Come in a new direction," we just need to step out and follow. Abraham just stepped out into omnipotence. That's not a bad thing to do. We need to make sure that we realize that separation is never from; it's always to. When God calls us to separate ourselves to His plan, we're never losing; we're gaining. We become dead to the world, but alive to God. That's where I want to be. Always remember, never doubt in the dark what God has shown you in the light. That was Abraham's secret. That was the secret through which hundreds of folks in our single adult ministry discovered "who He was" and "whose they are."

We know the promises that He's given us. We know who He is. Whether there are bright days or dark days, we don't want to get ahead of God or behind God. We don't want to doubt God or try to explain God. We don't want to be tempted not to believe, but we want to thrive in our belief and faith. With a burning desire more than ever to follow hard after God and the joy of watching God answer the needs in the lives of Single Purpose people, I discovered I was about to step into the steps He prepared for me as a Senior Pastor. As I said, some dark days, some bright days, but in all ways, He was there!

Chapter Nine

Some Bright Days, Then Dark Days But In All Ways He Was There

The Voyage Looked Wonderful

Some bright days, then dark days, but in all ways He was there. We had seen the hand of God and felt His power and presence work in the lives of the single adults at Neighborhood Church. The name Single Purpose had been chosen through the view of the fact that, for the born-again Christian, the most important thing in the life was to be in the center of God's Will. The Single Purpose is to acknowledge Him first in everything. As the Bible teaches and faith reveals, it is from that position that the power, purpose, and plans of God are unleashed in a life. This brings glory to Him and joy and fulfillment to the believer. The scripture that meant so much to us was Colossians 2:9-10, "For I am complete in Christ who is the head of all power and principality." The purpose of the single's life, as in everyone's life, was to allow the Holy Spirit to grow you through good and bad times alike to become all that God wants you to be. Your completeness would come in the fact that you belong to Him and He lives his life through you. Your marriage, your career, your family-everything needed to be placed in the middle of God's will.

It wasn't long until I discovered the Holy Spirit in the steps he'd prepared for me to become a Senior Pastor. These steps, as the chapter suggests, would have some bright days and dark days. But I found that in all ways, He was there with me. One of the former deacons at our Neighborhood Church had moved to the foothills of California and was ministering at a church that had a great probability of growth. It's location and situation could meet the needs of countless people. After visiting and preaching for the congregation, I went into a season of prayer to seek God's Will. I did not want to run ahead and launch a ship that wasn't prepared like Noah had when he built the ark. I didn't want to lean on what I thought I had learned and what God had allowed me to accomplish like the Titanic setting out on its ill-fated voyage. After much prayer and conversation with deacons, I accepted the call and we moved to the foothills of California. The move was difficult. The senior pastor at Neighborhood Church was like a second father to me. It was like leaving the comfort of a large established church to go to a place that would not have the balance, the years of ministry, the stability, and truly the spirit that Neighborhood had possessed. This new church had come through a difficult time and was looking to regroup and grow. The opportunity was exciting, challenging, and the benefits were very special. Our first new home was situated on a beautiful piece of land with a community that was looking for leadership and a church to grow. The church had a school and a small retirement center. The vision had been cast, but a team had not yet been put together. I asked God to help me remember what I had learned, what I had seen, what I had observed from great Godly men, and what God had taught me. On arriving in this new situation, we went about the first couple of years building a team, healing hurts, and growing a reputation for the church with a heart and an evangelical voice.

God began to bless in wonderful ways. The church began to grow. We were able after a time to bring in a youth pastor and then a minister of music. We prayerfully looked for ways to reach the community and modeled our Christmas and Thanksgiving programs after what we'd done at the Cathedral of the Cross Roads. I will never forget the first year we presented our version of "The Gloria." After addressing the congregation and singing an opening song, the curtains opened on a street scene in Bethlehem. As the crowd mingled in front of the shops, a shepherd walked across the crowded street into the open country (which was a backdrop). Upon closer observation, I saw that three of his sheep were fine, but his goat only had three legs, and hobbled along baaaaahing in what seemed to be a fit of delight. I tried to keep a straight face, but the full house audience began to quietly chuckle, openly laugh, and then loudly applaud. At this point, the shepherd nearing the end of the stage turned and politely bowed to the congregation . . . what a scene!

Although many people in the area said it couldn't be done, God was faithful. (To this day I am confident that He even used a three-legged goat.) It wasn't many years until we had a few thousand people from the foothills and the valley coming to see the Christmas story and Gloria at our church. The choir and music ministry, the youth ministry, our children's ministry, and our retirement home all began to nurture and grow leadership and reach out to the community.

Our youth minister was open and receptive. Together with sharing from past experiences from my life along with what God was doing in his life, we put together a youth ministry that not only blessed our church, but also set up a camp in another county that brought in students to the program from over a dozen other churches in the area. We were growing, training, and encouraging them to go back and commit their lives to Christ and change their towns and cities for the Lord. Our music minister expanded our Christmas and summer musical programs to the extent that our little church had a cast of over 100 involved. The cable television stations in the area began to see what was happening and asked if they could film and record our programs as well as feature our morning worship service on television to reach people throughout a three-to-four county area, a segment that not always could come to church on its own. We called the program "Come Alive!" Because you "come alive" when you commit your life to Jesus

Christ and it's He who puts life, purpose and meaning into your life and encompasses it with the joy of living with Jesus.

KFIA Christian Radio came to our service, observed it on television, and asked if they could broadcast us live for our Sunday morning worship service. Our board voted unanimously in favor of a live broadcast of our morning worship which covered all the foothills and much of northern California within a month. The program's title, "Come Alive," brought the ears unto the Holy Spirit and moved the hearts of countless people. Our prayers were being answered that lives would be changed, encouraged, strengthened and driven to a hunger for more of the Word.

There were many challenges, not to mention attitude changes. At times, some folks wanted to simply stay within the walls of the church. They were comfortable with things in the "Status quo mode." Finances were always close. In fact at this time, the San Francisco 49ers and head coach, Bill Walsh had developed something called the West Coast Offense. In football, that meant that QB Joe Montana would throw five-six yards with each completion. The "Niners" would move the ball down the field slowly, but steadily. We borrowed that name and applied it to our finance philosophy and our two boards. The West Coast Finances would prayerfully plan and implement what we could pay for. But we always kept the vision alive, or like the Niners, kept moving down the metaphoric field towards the goal that God was giving us! For we believed what scripture says, ". . . without a vision, the people perish." And the money, and the timing, and the results; well, those were in God's hands.

God was blessing and answering prayers. Lives were being saved. Committed Christians were being placed in ministries and the church's reputation as a family and heart-warming congregation was reaching out to three or four counties not to mention the radio and television coverage. We had prayerfully moved forward in our mission's vision with missionaries actively involved in Romania, Latvia, and the Soviet Union. These were missionaries we took care of directly through our church budgeting and congregational prayers and giving. Without going into a lot of exciting details, I felt in my heart that, by faith, I was watching God accomplish dreams, answer prayers, and meet needs in incredible ways. Thinking back to Hebrews 11 once again, I was beginning to feel a little bit like Jacob, when God told him in Genesis 32:28 that from then on, he would be called Israel which meant "Prince of God." Jacob had learned his lesson with God. I was just really beginning down that difficult road. Everything seemed to be going so great and unwittingly to my head. Though I never forgot who was giving the blessings, I wasn't hearing His voice as clearly as needed and I was seeking my own rules.

The Storm that Ended the Voyage

Do you remember times in your lives that everything seemed to be going in the direction that you prayed for? Where you felt like surely you were doing exactly what God wanted and all was well? Most of us can remember times like this in our life. It's been said that when times begin to be a little bit easier, sometimes we take our eyes off God. I believe that statement to be totally factual and instrumentally true as I look back in my life.

Sometimes when we're watching the hand of God paint the picture before our eyes and turn it into reality in the lives of people, we lose some of the close communion that is necessary and vital as we walk with the Savior. There had been many, many bright days, but now the darkest of dark days was coming. God would carry me through the darkest time of my life by faith in His faithfulness.

I made some bad decisions, bad choices, resulting in some life-changing decisions that I had to make. Once again I felt like Jacob, only in the pre-Israel name in his life! When I was rationalizing with God and unwittingly losing my connection in His will, I was reminded of a statement that my wonderful dad had told me years in the past. 'When you've done all you think and know to do, and then come to the Lord, you've done it backwards, Son. You need to come to Him first with no holds barred in your prayer life!" You see, that is what Jacob had done with the Lord as he struggled on the road to becoming renamed Israel by God. He said, "Lord, I have done all I know to do, so now I will have a little devotional time with you." It takes more than that to be in leadership for the Lord. In fact, it takes more than that to have a personal relationship and walk with the Lord! Jacob even tried to run from the Lord, but that was fruitless. I remembered trying to run from the voice of the Lord while singing in night clubs in Hawaii at a very young age as I mentioned earlier in this book. It didn't work then. It didn't work now. And it will never work for you, my friend.

Running, Jacob found himself in a place of desperation. Remember the story in Genesis? The angel wrestles with Jacob after He cripples him. The angel didn't want to let him go. We need to understand this. The Lord was saying in His heart, "I hope he doesn't." Have you ever noticed that about the Lord? He seems to act like He doesn't want to be there, but He really does. He wants us to walk in obedience! Even though I had disobeyed and rationalized my way around His truths, He was holding on to me, like the angel held on to Jacob.

As I thought about this, my mind went back to Jesus on the Amaeus road when He walked with those disciples. The Bible says He would have gone a little further, but they asked Him to stay there with them! He really wanted to stay, but He wanted them to want it and want Him! Looking back I am drawn again to the question He emblazoned across my heart and mind, "How much do you really want me?" As with Jacob, it was fixed fight and, as with Joe, God knew exactly what He was doing.

I grabbed hold of God that day in a way I never had before. I wanted Him to remove me from the place of desperation I had put myself in. I loved and wanted Him to have total control of my life in. I loved and wanted Him to have total control of my life. No longer would I depend on my sea-worthiness, scheming, begging, pleading, and bargaining or "I know God's mind" mentality. My heart's prayer would only be no more resistance, only reliance on Thee! Friend, whether we admit it or not, we tend to depend on other things along with God. He does not accept that! Where, or what, is it that you think of as your assisting power source? Could it be business ability, looks, personality, education, or music ability? Are you holding on to them? Or trusting only in Him?

The purpose of this book is not to delineate bad decisions, but rather to show a path by God's faithfulness to illustrate, alleviate, and elevate you over them in your life. I pray the Holy Spirit will enlighten you with direction and trust in what He can do to strengthen and revive you! The legitimacy of faith does not come by reading a book, but by walking through the valley of the shadow of death and finding out that He is there. That He holds your hand and carries you through. The unconditional love of God reaches far beyond the "man-made mistakes" that we make. He not only forgives, cleans, cleanses, but also restores in accordance with His omniscient timing and perfect will.

After meeting with key friends in ministry and spiritual leaders, it was prayerfully time to make choices again with Him! Led of the Lord, I resigned this church and stepped into the unknown. I thought about Jacob and how he wrestled with the Lord, and Abraham who by faith obeyed God and moved into the unknown. I was thankful for a God who loved me enough that He took my hand and walked me into the unknown even when it had not been complete obedience, but rather rationalized disobedience that had brought about the need.

Some bright days and some dark days . . .
but in all ways He was there.

Chapter Ten

The New Dawn

*The purpose of this book is not to delineate bad decisions,
but rather to show a path by God's faithfulness to illustrate,
alleviate and elevate you over them in your life.*

Moving into the Unknown

It seems I found myself in the very spot I had been 25 years earlier. About to move into the unknown and asking God what He would have me to do. Do you remember a time in your life where there was a complete change of direction in your life? Perhaps caused by others, or through others? Or even by decisions or choices that you made? In any event, you will know what I mean when I say that when the light goes out, it really gets dark. In the dark as I cried out to the Lord, He not only heard my prayers, but reminded me once again that light always enters and replaces the dark. Dark can never take away the light. I though back to an evening in my office at the church when it was a moonless night in the foothills and it was very dark. I had finished the letters and outlines I'd been working on and prepared to leave. It was a Wednesday night and, much to my surprise, the choir and everyone else had left the immediate campus. As I turned out the lights in my office to go to the side door which exited into the hall to leave the building, I realized just how dark my office was. In the darkness of my office, I walked toward the door and could see a slit of light coming up under it. Moving my way through the darkness, I didn't trip over a chair, step on a plant, or knock over a bookcase. When I reached the handle of the door and opened it, I watched the light from the hall slips its way into the darkness and illuminate a beam, a pathway, and a direction across my dark office. Little did I know at that time, but later I would remember that darkness and feel the hand of God's presence and direction because of it.

I had moved into the unknown. God reminded me that His light was there and would give a path of direction for His will and a call to whatever He wanted me to do. As the light came across my office floor late that dark night, His light fluttered across my heart. The peace that passes all understanding from John 14:27 flooded my soul! Part of that light God gave me as a wonderful brother-in-law in Steve Robinson and my sister, Evelyn. They are faithful servants of the Lord through whom God has blessed and touched the lives of thousands of people. Not feeling that I would be going back into the pulpit to preach or pastor, I began praying for God to show His light in the direction of what He would have me to do with my life and serving Him. It was at this point through conversation and prayer with Steve and Evelyn and my wonderful daughter, Amy Jo, that I followed God's leadership into Christian education. Years earlier, a doctor, a wonderful man by the name of Dr. Sam Rodriguez, came into my church and led teaching seminars for the certification of Christian school teachers for the State of California certification program. Sam was the head of the education program for Shasta Bible College and is a very dear friend to this day. We met and prayed and he, along with other pastors who were my friends, said "Joe, you should go into education and build lives in Christian schools." at that point, I began studying with Dr. Rodriguez and working on a master certification to teach. I remember Dr. Sam saying to Me, "Joe, you can tell how big a person is by what it takes to discourage him."

His Voice in the First Step

During this two-year period of working on my certification, I went to work in a public school as substitute teacher, using the credentials I had as a pastor. As I sought to draw close to the Lord at this time, I'll never forget perhaps the biggest turning point in my life to this very day. I'd been struggling with my decisions and seeking by faith-legitimate faith-God's daily direction while in my first substitute teaching job in the outskirts of Carson City, Nevada. I went into this modern, but rural school. As I entered into a sixth-grade classroom in an elementary school setting to substitute one afternoon, I understood that this group was totally foreign to me in this capacity. The teacher, a very nice young man, was excellent with children, but not very good with adults. He did not even have time to acknowledge me, being very rude. As he continued on the floor with the students and their class session, I found myself overpowered with this sense of anxiety. I made my way to the door, opened it, and stepped into the new modern hallway, which was inhabited by no one at that time, I leaned against the wall and as I began to break out into a cold sweat, my hands began to tremble. I cried out, "Lord, no one even knows I'm alive," I still vividly remember saying, "Lord, I've gone from a schedule every hour and all the hustle and bustle of the agenda I lived by to a place on the back side of the desert in which no one even knows I'm here." At that moment, I looked down and there stood a young lady with pigtails and freckles on her face. She was carrying a roll sheet it appeared. She stopped right in front of me, still bouncing with her ponytail, said to me, "Good morning, Mr. Teacher." Looking into her face, I said, "Well, how are you doing?" Are you having a good morning?" And she goes, "Yes sir, Mr. Teacher." And she skipped off. It was as if Jesus was standing right there with His hand on my shoulder, looking into my face saying, "Joe, you're partially right, but horribly wrong. Yes, nobody really knows you're here except me and it doesn't matter that they don't. It means everything that I do." I felt His touch on my shoulder and the presence and His peace in a miraculous way.

Soon after this I was called to teach at Dayton High School by the principal, Mr. Dave Regalato. He was a wonderful Christian man and we developed a warm and lasting relationship. We prayed together and Dave would say to me, "Joe, you were a fine pastor in the church. Now you are not preaching to the choir, you are reaching students in need of the Savior!" I was able to substitute teach in about every class that the high school offered. God gave me the opportunity to once again reconnect with both students and parents as I had in those wonderful years in youth ministry with Sonshine. Right there on the public school campus, I had the joy and privilege of encouraging students with Christian principles for living! Also, God allowed me to lead some students to the saving knowledge of Jesus Christ.

I will never forget my first real teaching day in the high school. I was covering for the senior English class and it was my first time. After praying for the Lord to give me insight and discernment, I seemingly fell on my face. A young man (an all-league wrestler and football defensive end) had developed and attracted his own special group of young ladies that was intent on studying him rather that the lesson left by their esteemed English teacher I was filling in for. After failed attempts at redirecting his and their attention to the class-known protocol and lesson, I asked him a question in front of everyone. "Chris, when you are ready to listen, you and the six young ladies around you will begin to learn." He immediately stood to his feet and said, "Who is going to make me?" I then proceeded to take three steps out from behind the lectern toward him when it hit me. What was I doing! He was already walking toward me! He was six-foot four and weighed about 235 pounds. Even though I was not accustomed to combative disrespect, I was headed down the wrong road.

As we met at the aisle, I said, "We will take this outside in the hall," at which point everyone in the class jumped out of their seats and fled to the walls of the classroom. I directed everyone to sit back in their respective seats and I opened the door for a huffing and puffing Chris. As we exited the room, I threw up a prayer of desperation. "Lord, please give me the words to say and the heart to hear . . . and let me live through this conflict!" Chris immediately butted his chest against me in the hall as the door closed. I asked myself, how could this senior hall be so empty at this moment?

As he starred in my face, I said, "Chris, if you feel that hitting a grandfather will make you more of a man, then give it your best shot!" Then I prayed, "O Lord don't let him hit me!"

Chris's facial expression changed as he said, "Grandfather?" At which point I said, "Absolutely," and pulling out my wallet said, "Would you like to see my grandkids?" He looked at my gang and said, "Hey, they are really cute." I said, "Chris, you are making me look bad and this is my first day here. And listen man, I don't really have a clue what I am doing yet." He began to crack a slight smile and I quickly proceeded to remember what Abraham Lincoln had said about leadership, "Etiquette and personal dignity are sometimes wisely set aside!" Lincoln also said, "Showing your compassionate and caring nature will aid you in forging successful alliances." I said, "Chris, I'll make you a deal. If you will help me with the class using your leadership ability, I will give you a great grade for the week." This touched the young man's heart . . .

As we re-entered the room, Chris hollered out, "Everyone sit down and shut up. Mr. Schofield has things to teach us and we need to learn!" Thus began a relationship that blossomed over that year. When I was asked to develop the first-ever summer school catch-up program for units needed for graduation, Chris ended up being enrolled in a literature class that I taught. On the first day of summer school, two rambunctious young men stood up in the last two rows and were about to come to blows at which point Chris fired out of his personally-selected chair in the front row and caught both men immediately. He held them by the neck, one in each hand (man, the kid was strong) and loudly to their faces said, "Hey, nobody fights in Mr. Schofield's class. Do you read me?" Total acceptance and complete responsibility followed from both fellas. You see, Chris came from a drug-fractured, untenable home and needed to know that God loved him. He also needed to be able to see it in somebody "with some skin" . . . me. God was reminding me of who He is and whose I was.

It was also during these days that God allowed me to meet and begin a prayer time with Mr. Mike Smith, the head engineer at Dayton High School. We had many wonderful times of prayer together for our lives, families and students at the school. God opened the door for me to have a prayer time with many of the teachers during the lunch breaks. Thank God, the Spirit of Jesus was in that place! As I continued to seek the Lord, Mike introduced me to Pastor Marvin Dennis of the Wesleyan Church in Carson City. He became a special friend and God opened the door for me to sing and preach for his church and the many students that went there. The Lord kept filling my heart with His peace and answering my questions with His Wisdom and His Word. As I look back, I am reminded of another thought-provoking, spiritual-enlightening phrase used by Mr. Zig Ziglar, "Don't put a question mark where God puts a period!" God was working in my life and, although I had a long way to go, the road was smoothing out with that assurance I spoke of ringing loudly in my heart.

His Lead in the Next Step

After completing the certification program with 60 hours of completed course work with Dr. Rodriguez, God opened the door to send me to the next part of His "training process" to show me a legitimate faith-faith with teeth, faith that would grip, faith that would hold, faith that not only would be unshakeable, but this time be immovable as well. The desire of my heart was to simply love God, love my family, and love people for His sake!

I received a phone call from a Christian international boarding high school in Oregon. After a wonderful conversation with its president, Mr. Doug Wead, I was hired as the principal of this school. Also, I was to pastor the campus church which reached out to the school community and to the surrounding town and area. This small town in Oregon was quite a change from what I'd come from.

Doug Wead had just finished a term on the White House Staff with President George Bush and had worked with George W. Bush, at that time the Governor of Texas. He had a heart for students and when 9/11 hit, we realized that the best way to fight terrorism was to send young men and women back to their countries who were born again, loved God, and could bring the love of God to their people. We had students from 14 nations around the world, and 9 of the contiguous 48 states. In my quiet times and devotions with God I continued to ask Him, "God, what exactly would you have me do and how could I get through to each of the students with none of me, but all of you?" It was a totally new world to me with totally new challenges. Things that I'd felt so inept at, God always gave ways to not only succeed, but also to touch and change lives. Speaking of feeling totally inept, upon meeting the first parents of our Japanese students as they bowed and I tried to bow back, I actually bumped heads, which if it weren't for being a Christian school would be such a horrible thing, but instead actually enabled us to shake hands and draw close.

Can you recall times in your life where God has redirected you or you found yourself in a totally new world? The Lord, your love for Him, and his faithfulness are the same, but any semblance of understanding or any feeling of capability has been stripped from you? You needed to learn the entire rules of the game almost on a daily basis to fulfill what God had asked you to do that day? Then you too will agree with me that His presence is sweeter and more wonderful than you could have ever imagined. And as you walk with him through the dark days and the bright days, the grey days and the great days, He is more wonderful every day.

At this school, I had the privilege and the blessing of God to meet Congressman Dave Weldon and his wife, Nancy. They brought their daughter to be a part of our school community. And I learned again the sweetness of prayer when Dave and Nancy prayed with my wife and me. Dave shared of the great directional change in his life from being a medical doctor in Florida to a United

States Congressman, working closely with stem cell research under President George W. Bush. But as Dave always said, God is always and always will be faithful when we look to Him. It made me think of that old phrase, "There's nothing you can do to make God love you more; nothing you can do to make him love you less. God just loves you." And when I prayed with Dave, we felt just how much God loved us. We also watched the Lord calm the 9/11 fears and encourage the hearts of my students, faculty and staff! We had all watched in horror on a common large-screen television the fateful events of that morning. I had cancelled all classes and brought everyone together to have community and prayer. God replaced the fear with His assurance and the peace of His presence.

You may read about His presence, but when you experience and see it in the faces of those around you, it reveals reality and you really "get it."

Through a series of events, I ended up beginning a brand new high school in the capital of Oregon. Dr. Sam Rodriquez came up from California to help me as assistant administrator and was such a great leader, brother, and prayer partner. I'd never been more excited in what God was accomplishing through wonderful people such as Doctors Ralph and Jo Hill. They had also become family for my wife and me. Prayers, support, and friendship through great knowledge and wisdom were continually flowing to me from this precious couple. From his wonderful stories of events on New Guinea and the Marianna Islands, where he was in charge of unloading ships in WWII, to the relationship of those stories to the students and families we dealt with at the school, Ralph was always a source of laughter and blessing. I thank God for the way he watched over my health and the tips he gave on just about every part of life from his vast experience. As we prepared to break ground at a brand new Christian high school with a $2.5 million piece of land, I was just beginning to wonder what God would do next. That December, I got sick with a cold and it would not go away. As I spoke in churches each weekend, promoting the new high school and meeting the students and families in this temporary location, I was told by my good friend and doctor that I had developed a lung disease purportedly due to the damp mold and cold in my lungs. Growing up in a warm climate, living in Oregon had an adverse effect on my lungs. At this time I began to ask the Lord, "OK Lord, what's next? What's new? Whatever it is, I'm with you." As Zig would say, "Don't give God instructions; just report for duty."

Being told I could not live in that climate if I wanted to breathe and, since breathing is an important part of life, I prayerfully put out a resume in the direction of Texas and said, "Lord, wherever you say, we're ready and we'll go."

His Strength in the Big Step

Though my faith was a little shaky at this point, I had two thoughts that continually drew me back to God and the joy of His presence. Friends, I had disappointed Him before and I didn't ever want that to happen again. Also, He was so faithful to me through it all. I knew He loved me and would never let anything happen to me that would not please Him or be in His Plan for my life. My life was all about Him, and He had me in His grip.

I received a call from many Christian schools and in particular I was moved and touched by Faith Christian High School in Grapevine, Texas. In talking with Dr. Ed Smith, the President, Rev. John Brooks, the Chaplain, and Mr. Jeff Potts, the Principal, I knew as Romans says, "my spirit bore witness with their spirit" that faith was on God's agenda for my life.

We not only belonged to the Lord, but we also felt the same call. God is incredible to do His work. In a period of six weeks, God sold our home to one of our students and his new wife from two years prior in the high school when I was their principal. This allowed us to bless them. We packed up and moved all the way from Oregon to Texas. God planted me in a wonderful Christ-centered Christian school and faculty. Yes, it was a big step.

Upon arriving in Ft. Worth, we had the pleasure of reuniting with my sister, Jeani Beth, and her husband, Pastor Cliff Poe. It had been 32 years since I had the joy of uniting them in marriage in Glendale, California. They are very special people and our prayers together were wonderful. When reporting for my new position at Faith Christian, I began to teach Bible and work in administration with summer program and ministry toward the new high school that was being built. As we studied God's word, prayed with students and families, God gave me the most precious time I had experienced to that point in my life. I had no kingdoms to build, no programs to launch, no worldwide ministries that I needed to create. I only needed to love God, love my family, love people, and ask Him daily to allow my life to make a difference for eternity, for someone else. At Faith Christian, I prayerfully became a part of the core value and statement we all strove to live by-"To develop and create authentic Christian leaders." The prayer of my heart was that my life would emulate and show forth an example of what that should be like. I would often tell students, "Gang, whoever crosses your path today ought to be a better and more loved person because they spent a few moments with you, not because of who you are, but whose you are!" Peer pressure in high school (as in all of life) may be relegated to a very minor position when we live our lives to an audience of one-the Lord Jesus Christ!

Dear friend, can you remember in your life when everything took on a new priority? When God's direction became so clear because it was all about Him and not at all about you? Maybe you're facing questions right now in your life with what you want to be doing and what you feel He wants you to do. My prayer for you is that you would see as we did that it's one day at a time, lifting everyone else around you.

My mind went back to Dr. Clarence Sands years earlier and what he'd told me once when he preached from Philippians 2. His sermon was "The Way Up is the Way Down." When you lift everyone else around you, they will pull you with them to God. Or as stated my dear friend, Zig Ziglar, whose life's motto was "When you help someone else achieve what God wants in their life, you achieve the peace that He gives which will give you your heart's desire in return."

As I watched God work in the lives of students and families and my life was enriched by their joy, enthusiasm and love, I received a wonderful phone call from a friend of mine from 40 years past in my college days. His name-Dr. Jack Graham. I heard his voice saying, "Man, what are you doing?" It was like stepping back to those formative years when I gave my heart to Christ. It was a flash to the past and guess what? God was there!

I went to visit Jack and we had lunch in the church cafe at Prestonwood Baptist Church where Jack was now the pastor. Once again I felt the Lord speak to me, this time through my friend of over 40 years. We reminisced about times at Hardin-Simmons University- shooting hoops in the old Marston Gymnasium, events in Tau-Alpha Fi fraternity, how he met his wife, Deb, and the times when the two of us had spent time into the wee hours of the morning, praying on our little back porch in the HSU married housing colony there in West Texas. After going to Prestonwood and hearing my brother Jack Graham preach, we joined the church. It was during the ensuing months that Jack reminded me and the Lord whispered in my heart that I had been called to preach, teach, and to be a pastor. I quietly prayed with my good friend, Mr. Nolan LaBeaux, the junior high principal at my beloved Faith Christian. Then I went to prayer with special brother, John Brooks, and then my close friend and boss, Dr. Ed Smith. Even though I had another year with stipulations on my FCS contract, Ed said, 'Joe, you need to follow the Lord's open door and call to Prestonwood." Once again I was blessed and touched by Faith Christian School, a place that had loved me and allowed me to minister and grow in God's grace. Dr. Ed Smith will always be one of the "mile marker men" that God used to love and lead me through. He is a quiet, deeply spiritual and always relevant friend!

His Peace in the Final Step

Friend, my choices at one point had deterred me from that call. His unconditional love, patience, and faithfulness, was about to move me from His training/restoration ground in education back to the pulpit and the pastoral life to minister to people.

I was extended the call to become the Associate Pastor and Minister to Adult 4 and 5. This encompassed the boomers and the seniors of Prestonwood.

Prestonwood Baptist Church
Plano, Texas

Over the next several years, I would see God move me into the ministry to wonderful senior adults and the countless numbers of people that are part of the boomers reaching that special age in life, an age that is searching for answers as never before. The realization that the time to deal with the questions God had been asking for so many years had arrived indeed! As one distinguished gentleman said to me, 'Joe, it is not that I ever really turned my back on God. I just never had time for Him. Now the Holy Spirit was compelling me to find the answers that I have so long run from, but are so critically important and of eternal significance!" He went on to say, "I am loved and respected by my wife, my children, and grandchildren. They think I have all the answers and I want to let them know that at last I do!" I had never been more excited about the opportunity God had given me to serve Him than I was at this point in my life! Every eight seconds, someone will turn 60. What a special opportunity from God to make an eternal difference in the lives of countless people!

As I looked in the mirror and looked at those special people, I realized that God had taken me once again full circle. He was giving me the privilege of prayerfully working with that wonderful group of people that I lovingly call, "Those of us who have been younger longer." People perhaps like you who've come down a road in life with your eyes on Christ, but have sometimes made choices that put a pothole in the road and a diversion in your life. Perhaps you've come through difficulties where you've wondered where God was, only to discover that He never left you. You had just lost the signal.

Coming to Prestonwood thrilled my soul and blessed me beyond measure. Leaving Faith Christian was difficult as I loved those people and they had blessed my life immeasurably. But moving back into the roles of pastoral ministry had given me a whole new insight from what I ever would have had before. God's blessings have been innumerable. One very special blessing is the introduction to, close bonding with, and love I have for Mr. Zig Ziglar and his wonderful wife, Jean. Zig continued to learn from the Lord through him that real faith-legitimate faith-does not come from reading a book, or trying to be someone you're not, or modeling your life to be something you think you should be. Rather it is putting your hand in the hand of the Lord and simply following Him one day at a time.

Legitimate faith grows from the seed bed of God's unconditional love and everlasting faithfulness. The weeds of your poor choices may be used by Him to complete His plan for your life. And the fruit of your growth is the peace that passes understanding where it's anchored in the assurance of who the Lord Jesus Christ is, what he has done for you, and how He holds you in the grip of His grace when you obediently look to Him. The prayer of my life now is that, through my life, God will help me to help others out of potholes, out of darkness, and into His light. Also, that I can help people discover the joy of God's forgiveness, the completeness of His grace, and the wonderful call to obedience and what that produces in a relationship with Jesus.

My prayer is that you seek Him in such a way that you just get all of you out of the way and let Him take complete control of your life. Perhaps you need to come to the place where you say, "I have no kingdoms to build, no ships to sail, no planes to launch. I am not embarrassed. I am not ashamed. I am not afraid. My sins are under the shed blood of Jesus and all is right between Him and me!"

I humbly believe the Lord has placed me in the palm of His hand that he might set me right before you as a voice of encouragement, a hand for direction, and a heart that cries out to tell you that God loves you beyond what you think you could ever know. It's my prayer that you'll get beyond what you've learned and get into what He can show you. That you won't be a "been there, know that, done that" individual but instead, a "can't wait to see" desire to know, and humbly ready to receive all that He will give you for His glory.

Legitimate faith produces a legitimate life that through Christ will produce encouragement and joy in all of those around you to the glory of God until he comes for you. You may give them the road map to life in order that they may discard the worldly directions for mere existence!

Please remember, Hebrews 11 has shown us clearly through the lives of men and women who struggled, who learned, and who grew. Faith is the assurance of things hoped for and the conviction of things not seen. May you be at a place in your life where you can say, "Through the Lord Jesus Christ I have seen the things I've hoped for which have given me the assurance and conviction of the things that I couldn't see."

He has been faithful beyond belief; I will be faithful with my belief. Friend, don't waste your sorrows, broken homes, broken hearts, and broken spirits. If we are smart, we will save ourselves from future wrestling matches with God like Jacob went through. We may rest and lean on Jesus by faith, as Jacob rested and leaned on his staff in the full blessing of God. (Hebrews 11:21)

May we be able to stand before Him and have Him say, "Well done, my good and faithful servant." And may people behind us remember us for our faithfulness. As the hymn says, ". . . may those who come behind us find us faithful."

Legitimate faith = legitimate life = legitimate eternity-all through a personal relationship with Jesus Christ.

Reprise
WILL YOUR ANCHOR HOLD?

As I have perused my life in a high altitude review, it has caused me not only to evaluate who God is and what He has done in loving response in my journey of learning, but also to ask myself "What have I learned?"

God is always faithful to His promises. Though He doesn't always work things out the way we think He should, His ways are not our ways. They are the right way! Very often God will prove His faithfulness to us through extreme adversity by providing just what we need to survive; then turning on the lights at just the right time. He does not change our painful circumstances whether we caused them or not, but rather He sustains and grows us through them. Again, the writer to the Hebrews amplifies this truth in Hebrews 4:16.

*"Let us therefore draw near with confidence to the
throne of grace, that we may receive mercy and may
find grace to help in time of need."*

This gives us such a needed promise! When we are in need,
God will, among other things, provide us with mercy and grace.
I continue to learn that all the "other things" are brought forth
through, and because of, His mercy and grace! When Paul had
the difficult "thorn in the flesh," God chose to sustain him through
it rather than to remove it. "My grace is sufficient for you." (2
Corinthians 12:9) Can you remember times in your life when God
has quietly whispered those words in your ears as you were seeking
and praying for His direction, forgiveness and gentle touch? When
the lights had gone out and you couldn't find the switch?

May I encourage you to think with me and with yourself in
mind as I close with perhaps the most valuable and reassuring
message my loving Heavenly Father has given to me? With a heart
that always wanted to be close to Him, I was often found in that
"battle of the ages" that is clarified in the "battle of the natures"
found in Romans 6 and 7.

As the Apostle Paul so aptly phrased it in Romans 7:15 when
he said, "I do not understand my own actions. For I do not do
what I want, but I do the very thing I hate." He goes on to claim
the victory in Jesus in Verses 16-25 ". . . who will deliver me from
this body of death? Thanks be to God through Jesus Christ our
Lord . . ."

That is the reason I have written this humble book. Faith-
Legitimate Faith is always the victory! God wants that message
to be alive and pounding in the hearts of all of His people. The
victory was won at Calvary, and that comes alive in me (and you)
by, through, and because of our faith. Friend, may I please leave
you with a final thought that I pray will weave its way into your
mind and heart to encourage and strengthen you today?

From Then . . . Til Now

Growing up in Southern California I loved the ocean. Many times my Dad and I would fish there together and later in my teens I would surf there with my friends. When I was Associate Pastor with the Single Purpose ministry in Castro Valley, I had the opportunity to sail on San Francisco Bay with our minister of music and a special deacon who would "get us away" occasionally to rest and relax. He had a Catalina 27- foot sailboat that we sailed on, and we always had the same routine. We would sail out of Berkeley boat harbor and set out across the bay to Angel Island. There we would anchor down and lay back in the sun, chatting and then inevitably napping after devouring our deli-sandwiches followed by salt-vinegar potato chips. Doesn't that sound wonderful? OK, so it wasn't very healthy, but it was such a relaxing time.

One time a large ship went by rather close and a wave from its wake caused our little sail boat to toss up and down rather vigorously and I awoke from my nap. My brothers didn't budge, but I found myself staring at the anchor and its line that was tied off on our craft. I am reminded as we have thought about my life, faith, and in doing so followed the folks in the great faith chapter of Hebrews 11, . . . that the word "hope" in Hebrews 11:1 is also found in Hebrews 6:19-20 and refers to "the anchor of our soul." These verses tell us what it is and what it does. "We have this as a sure and steadfast anchor of the soul, a hope that endures into the inner place behind the curtain, where Jesus has gone as a forerunner on our behalf, having become a high priest forever after the order of Malchizadek." ESV

Throughout Chapter 6, the writer of Hebrews explains the distinctive power of that hope! Even here, he gives the example of God's faithfulness to Abraham and reminds us that He is a God and Father who makes and keeps His promises. Our purpose in life is to be centered in Christ. We will experience His judgment and reconciling love in Jesus Christ. His promise is that we can take an honest look at our lives and receive power to dare to be different and the encouragement that is anchored in His unconditional love and forgiveness. Christ is our anchor and a sure and steadfast anchor is dependable, safe and worthy of our trust.

I have asked myself so many times along with Paul, why did I do this or that? Why didn't I understand better what was happening? Why did I not seem to learn a lesson better than I did? Why did I drift in the winds of difficulty or move in the wrong direction on the waves of deception?

Friends, though we may believe in Christ, our anchor and the anchorage and grip that He has on our lives, sometimes we are not held firmly because the anchor line may have come loose on the ship! Just like I stared at the line from our little sailboat that kept us secure as the large transport went by, I had to tie it off on our craft.

May I give you another thought that struck me and now encourages me incredibly? The end of an anchor line is called by sailors, "the bitter end." It has to be tied down through the chocks (loops) along the top side of the deck, down into the hull, and tied to the mast. The worst thing that could happen would be this. The ship's end of the anchor line could come loose so that both the anchor and the anchor line would be lost in the sea! Now we may see why the ship's end of the line is called the bitter end. Can you imagine the fear that would grip you in rough water if you suddenly saw the bitter end skipping across your deck, flipping through your chocks, down the side of your hull and slipping into the sea?

That, I believe, is how we sometimes feel in life when we go through those faith-legitimizing storms. Our anchor is secure, but we somehow feel disconnected from it! We may be visualizing that line slipping away.

Sometimes when the winds of adversity, failed promises, and waves that destroy homes and fracture families occur, there is a "tug" on the anchor line in our hearts that reminds us we are secure. Just like the tug on the kite line I mentioned in an earlier chapter. We know He is there and His love is unconditional and powerfully redirectional as we grow! He is, and always will be, faithful!

Now spiritually, these tugs also remind us that we are accountable to God and through Christ forgiven and strengthened to move ahead innewness of life, encouragement, and growing faith! Sometimes it is in a new direction that we are now able to understand and "move out" to do! Remember the wonderful words of Jesus when He said in John 15:5,

> "I am the vine; you are the branches. Whoever abides in me and I in him, he it is that bears much fruit, for apart from me you can do nothing."

Sometimes we need to be reminded of "the graft" that was made when we received Jesus as our personal Savior and understand the vine we comprise may have taken a new direction. But is still filled with the same sap-our wonderful love of God and empowerment of the precious Holy Spirit! Our errors and poor decisions may at times produce a gnarly vine, but God is faithful and will produce a fruit that is divine!

From Now 'Til Then and . . . He Comes Again!

So I close by saying legitimate faith teaches us to always ask ourselves, "Is there anything I am attempting to do in my own strength? Am I trying to live the Christian life in my own way, or as others think I should be living it? Am I tired out, burned out, and just flat worn out?"

If so, then may I stop, prayerfully re-evaluate and live by the love, lessons, and presence of God that I have learned over the many years. Through all I have shared in this little book and so much more, I have emerged with a greater sense of and greater love for my Lord and Savior Jesus Christ! I understand deep in my soul His commitment to me and all His children. I know He is ever faithful, can always be trusted, and will be sufficient in all ways in every need. I still find that astounding and frankly beyond the realm of my human understanding. How does He love me and forgive me like He does?

Those wonderful things that have taught and given me a "Legitimate Faith" have been chiseled out of the stones of my life by an all-powerful God who is my loving heavenly Father and the "anchor of my soul." It is a wonderful fact that Christ holds us accountable and loves us enough to never let us go! He always understands and consequently tugs on that anchor line. He reminds me that He is mine and I belong to Him, now and forevermore.

Maybe you find yourself in a difficult circumstance of your own making, or one beyond your control. Whether God chooses to immediately take you out of the situation or leave you there for a season, He will walk you through and meet you at the deepest points of your needs while you are there. In fact, God said, "Peace I will leave with you. Not as the world gives do I give to you. Let not your hearts be troubled, neither let them be afraid." (John 14:27)

He will be faithful to protect you and sustain you until "His Perfect Will" is completed. In the process, His forgiveness and faithfulness will become gloriously evident to you each day in both beautiful and powerful ways! There is no safer place to be in time and eternity than to be resting in the palm of His hand. Remember, God did not say to Paul, "My grace will be sufficient for you," or "My grace has been sufficient for you." He said "My grace is sufficient for you!"

Dear friend that is in the present tense right where we live. Though my life has so many things I would change if I could, He has used everything for His glory and my growth. He has answered prayer time after time in His way and in His timing! His sufficiency has jumped off the pages of His word and has become reality in my life! I pray you know what I am talking about and, together, we may say with the Apostle Paul, "Therefore I will boast all the more gladly of my weaknesses, (yes, and my failures) so that the power of Christ may rest upon me."

Zig Ziglar is often heard to lovingly say, "I never worry. Don't worry about anything. Why should I when I've already won!" That's faith. That's legitimate faith!

As my Encouragers Bible Fellowship Class (which I thank God for every day) recently said to me on a special anniversary card with the words of John Milton, "The end of learning is to know God, and out of that knowledge to love Him and imitate Him."

Now, I ask you, what more encouragement and assurance could I (we) ever ask for than that! Legitimate Faith is the ever growing, trust-producing product of whose we are and how He loves us! "Blessed are they that put their trust in Him!" Psalm 2:12

Questions you may want to ask yourself. These are always in the center of my mind and personal prayer times as I need to stay on track!

1. Are you thirstier for God than ever before? (Psalms 42:1)
2. Do you love more each day? (1 John 4:7)
3. Is your life lived more by God's words each day? (2 Timothy 3:16-17)
4. Do you care for the spiritual and physical needs of others? (Luke 19:11)
5. Are the disciplines and habits of your life more Christ centered as you follow and grow in His Grace? (1 Timothy 4:7)

6. Are you constantly more aware of your sins? (1 Timothy 1:15)
7. Are you much more able to forgive others! (Ephesians 4:32)

In the words of the old song,

"Now I belong to Jesus, Jesus belongs to me!
Not for the years of time alone But for Eternity!"

ADDENDUM:
LEGITIMATE FAITH 2022

As I write this addendum to my book 'Legitimate Faith', some eight years later from the first of two requested re-publications, I realize that God has been so very faithful in His promises, proved by His presence, and joy. I also discovered that His greatest lessons were most often learned in my 'valley experiences', and not my 'mountaintop retreats'? It is adversity that reveals our strengths and weaknesses. We see this vividly portrayed in Judges 6:12-13, when Gideon learned that God was in control and His strength was in the Lord. There is no comparison between human strength and the might and ability of Almighty God. He is infinite and I am finite. He is with us in the everyday battles that we all face.

Throughout His word, He tells us, and in our lives, He literally shows us that in the pain, discouragement, feelings of hopelessness and suffering - He is there! No matter how difficult, He will turn adversities and fear into ever growing, upward levels of faith (Mark 4:35-41). We learn that fear always walks alongside adversity. In fact, it is that accompanying fear that makes just another experience become an adversity. Fear may shake us to our very, core so we expect the worst is bound to happen, and we will never recover . . . all is lost!

Friends, that is not what Legitimate Faith shows us in our lifelong trek with God. Instead, we see and experience that He really is in control. When we place our trust in Him, He is working in it all, that all of the above mentioned and so much more, will work out for our good (Romans 8:28). He shows us that we will make it, we will recover, and our faith will grow. Adversity and fear are replaced with ever raising expectations and a fresh desire to observe and experience the power and faithfulness of Almighty

God each day! Perhaps best of all, the more you use your faith, the greater it grows! He raises your expectations as you trust and 'walk it through' with Him. It becomes legitimate faith that is tried, tested and true in God's power, for His glory, and your fulfilled life!

In the last two and a half years, I have endeavored to follow in legitimate trusting faith, God's all upon my life. I have watched Him at work in my personal victories and very difficult defeats, from which I ran the cycle of the afore said struggles, praying 'what to do now'? It's not only seeing what to do, but how do you do it? Better said, how does God want you to do it? Should I move ahead in my experience, knowledge and understanding as a man, and just get it done, or should I stay on my knees and seek Him for the answers and directions for what I knew He was asking me to do! I am glad to say that the later was the route, and lessons learned became the directions taken, and the Holy Spirit took control!

God, through a series of events that were simply impossible to create, yet alone understand, opened the door and called me to create a new radio/tv show. I was to prayerfully think through and carefully build a show that would touch lives in unique and special ways. A show that would break down barriers and produced a family and friendly atmosphere for all who would tune in and watch! A show that would encourage people in the everyday things of life, showing them how to laugh and have the joy of friendship, realizing that God loves them and gave them His only begotten son to die for their sins . . . that they could have Eternal Life and LIFE NOW in this crazy, hurtful and disassociated world in which we live.

The real Good News . . . someday we will go to heaven (John 14), but until then we will have a life with peace, meaning, and unique direction from God's presence and power, each day and every way. The Bible says 'peace that passes understanding' (John 14:27), will continually and in so many different ways, Raise our

Expectations daily! This will create a fulfilling life not dependent upon circumstances, but quite often in spite of them! This is peace that will take fear out of adversities, because we know we will recover, and God will take that problem or difficult circumstance and use it for our good!

So, I prayerfully began the weekly radio/tv show 'Raising Expectations!' God led me to reach out and build a team of Co-Hosts to show a loving family uplifting and working together each week. What a blessing they have been to me and countless people in our audience each week!

Beginning with my college, lifelong friend, fellow pastor and brother in Christ, Dr. Paul Hall. God has used Paul to bless my life as we ministered together in college, seminary and years as pastors. Now, he is also a blessing to our whole team and all who see and hear him each week on the show! From his deep love for the Lord and His word, Paul gently tears down walls and displaces fears as our audience listens and watches each week. I thank God for Paul and the wisdom and support he has given me for over fifty years in ministry.

Then the Lord brought Top Gun trainer and F-14 pilot and squadron leader, Commander Rob Hansen and his wonderful wife Nancy. Rob is a graduate of the Naval Academy at Annapolis, and his knowledge of American history, political science and military tactics gave great insight to our shows. Rob's knowledge, leadership and love for God, Nancy, and people, has been a special blessing and encouragement to all of the team and listening friends. Nancy added that special touch of encouragement and grace each time she shared her thoughts. They are a special team, and I thank God for them!

Then, as God works, I received a phone call from Stephanie Thayer (renowned health and wellness coach) who, as a part of her business, was reaching out to help older pastors take are of their health! I thank God that I was in pretty good health! In her conversation, she shined in her Christian faith, introduced me to her wonderful husband Dr. Craig Thayer (an incredible trauma surgeon), and they teamed up with us to help share hope, encouragement and great faith in God each week. From nutrition to home-schooling, to parenting to Faith, our 'dynamic duo' in Christ blesses the team and audience every time we are on the air! I thank God for them!

On the recommendation of the Honorable Allan B. Clark (West Point graduate, war hero and presidential advisor to George HW Bush), I met Pastor Ron Greer (Regional Director for 'Man in the Mirror' Men's Discipleship Ministry across America). When I contacted Ron, a former pastor, I immediately know why Allan recommended him to me. What a delight he is as he weekly shares his wisdom and insights with us from his great faith and love the for the Lord. He is an integral part of our Co-Host team, and I thank God for him!

Week after week, we discuss Faith, Freedom, Family, Finances, and all the parts included therein, with special guests who are leaders in their fields. We take your questions and share insights and truthful, factual knowledge leading towards the greatest source of and guiding force in control . . . God.

Friends, we listen, we share, we care and we pray . . . and we ask God to take it from there, which is what He does best!!

Pastor Joe Schofield
Raising Expectations
bbsradio.com/Raising Expectations

The Boys of BBS Radio TV

I thank God for Don and Doug Newsome. As twin brothers and Co- founders of BBS Radio/ TV, they have become like sons to me with their guidance and support for my "Raising Expectations!" show each week. They have been in my prayers since we began two and one half years ago as of June 20/20!

Don's son T.J. has been a wonderful engineer for us and the kindness, respect and attention he gives us on the show is simply outstanding.

Again, I thank God for the gift of Doug, Don and TJ in my life as they help me pursue "His calling" and plans for my life in these senior adult years.

Guys- I love and appreciate you and your family. You will always be in my heart and prayers daily, as (with your help and kindness) we follow Gods plan to help people "Raise their Expectations!" in all areas of their lives by discovering the Love of God as shown for us in Jesus Christ His Son!

Thank you my friends!
Pastor Joe

A Word from Doug & Don

"In our lives we've encounter hundreds of thousands of unique individuals! In fact, we've produced over 100,000 hours of web-tv and radio programing for over 1,000 different hosts over the past two decades. We know new media! We understand it's significance! We were one of the first two companies in the United States to create live, interactive, internet broadcasts and podcasts, and mas syndicate those productions to the world. We've handled hosts from every continent and covered almost every subject imaginable! Indeed, BBS Network, Inc., known as BBS Radio TV, has been a pioneer in the new media industry, providing interesting, relevant, empowering, and original programming that changes lives and broadens the horizons of possibilities. We love what we do, and we truly care about this magnificent World and the lives of our listeners. Check out https://bbsradio.com, we'll be your favorite!

*Given our long prominence and vast connections, we know people, but there are those that come into our life that shine more bright than others, that embody love and awareness at a higher level; that mark them keenly as a beautiful soul; that make an indelible mark upon this earth. One such man is Pastor Joe Schofield. Joe's show, Raising Expectations, confronts us with issues on a national, political, and worldwide level, that affect our conscious and unconscious personal decisions! It is informative, inclusive, interesting, and always encouraging, and best of all, it strives to raise our expectations, to create a more positive future.

Everyone at BBS Radio TV knows Pastor Joe personally! We are most fortunate to call him a friend, and we earnestly pray you discover why that is . . . Tune in every Monday night at 9:00pm eastern time: https://bbsradio.com/raisingexpectations."

By Douglas Newsom and Donald Newsom, founders of BBS Radio TV

"Raising Expectations" Media

esident Ronald Reagan 6/
g Wead

Author Doug Wead with President Trump

MY WALL OF GRATITUDE

God often "fleshes out" His direction and shows His love through unique and wonderfully special people in our lives. These would be inclusive of those through whom God has clarified, encouraged, strengthened and taught me more of Himself throughout the many years. As I have often said, we as Christians are to be the visible proof of our invisible Savior until He comes again. These are the ones for whom I prayed and will forever be beholding and upholding their memory and names!

1. Rev. Donald K. Schofield & Lucille Jean Schofield (My Dad and Mom)
    A man of honor and integrity and a woman of constant love and support. Together they gave me wisdom, love, and modeled God's truths daily before me. I am blessed.

2. Ouida and Joe Robbins
    You would never know that they were not my real grandparents for they were that and so much more through their Christian strength and guidance. They loved like Jesus!

3. Dr. John McArthur
    Even as my youth pastor, the wisdom and heart for God that blesses countless thousands today, gently nurtured my life even then. Bold, courageous, and fearless to stand up in faith for Christ.

4. Dr. Clarence Sands
    One of God's most choice servants through whom God's truths were modeled as well as taught . . . forever instilling what the phrase "pastoral love" means. To this day, Doc's

picture hangs on my wall, smiling at me, and inspiring me to listen to what the Holy Spirit is saying.

5. Mr. Steve and Evelyn Robinson
   My wonderful sister and her husband, my lifelong friend. Both pillars of strength and Godly support in times of great storms. They walk the walk and talk the talk. Steve you have been my best friend and confidant. I am so very blessed!

6. Rev. Cliff and Jeani Poe
   My special sister and caring brother-in-law. Though years and miles apart, we have such a special bond of love in our hearts. Thanks for sharing insight and perspective with years of prayers. It's like we were always there together.

7. Dr. Paul Hall
   Paul you have been as a brother to me since our college and seminary days together! Your spiritual depth, love and discernment are priceless to me!

8. Andrea Kelly
   She is the most special lady in my life who prays for and constantly encourages me to follow God's directions and call for my life!

9. Drs. Ralph and Jo Hill
   A gift from God at a time of great need. Two wonderful people that gave an entire new meaning to the words "love and support."

10. Rev. Doug Wead
    A friend who shared great insight and perspective in understanding people and places.

11. Dr. Ed Smith

    A special blessing from God with the understanding of life and faith. I learned more each day about the way God gives a calm spirit. Ed is the eye of the hurricane.

12. Rev. John Brooks

    There could be no greater student chaplain than my dear brother. Thanks, John for your love, friendship and for helping me (like the example you shared) as John Wooten used to say, "Find my spot on the court."

13. Dr. Jack Graham

    One of God's greatest voices through whom God has spoken to me, strengthened me, and reminded me that He had a job for me. Jack, love you brother. Thanks for being who you are in my life!

14. Mr. Zig Ziglar

    The world knows you're the greatest encourager ever! I thank God and am humbled as I do so for the gift of your friendship and mentorship in my life. Thank you for being the inspiration and example you are to me. You, Sir, and Jean are simply the best!

15. Mr. Ron Kelley

    You give a whole new meaning to the phrase "Christian Brother." Trust, openness, caring, and just plain fun! I thank God for who you are in my life. My Buddy!

16. Rev Jeff Young and Greg McNeece

    I thank God for who you both are in your faith and leadership in ministry for our Savior. Each of you gives me a peace in my heart that when God calls me home, His ministry will be going strong through you. Your hearts are for the Savior and that makes it great to be on your team!

17. The Encouragers Class
   A never-ending source of encouragement, love and sweet fellowship. You are a special blessing and constant validation of the love of Christ in my life!

*   *   *   *   *